The Active Life

Other Books by Parker J. Palmer

The Company of Strangers: Christians and the
Renewal of America's Public Life

The Promise of Paradox: A Celebration of
Contradictions in the Christian Life

To Know As We Are Known: A Spirituality of
Education

The Active Life

A Spirituality of Work, Creativity, and Caring

Parker J. Palmer

1817

Harper & Row, Publishers, San Francisco

New York, Grand Rapids, Philadelphia, St. Louis
London, Singapore, Sydney, Tokyo, Toronto

Martin Buber, "The Angel and the World's Dominion," reprinted by permission of the translator, Jerome Rothenberg, from *Tales of Angels, Spirits, and Demons,* published by Hawk's Well Press, 1959.

Thomas Merton, *The Way of Chuang Tzu.* Copyright © 1965 by the Abbey of Gethsemani. Reprinted by permission of New Directions Publishing Corporation.

Julia Esquivel, "They Have Threatened Us With Resurrection," from *Threatened With Resurrection.* Copyright © 1982 by The Brethren Press, Elgin, IL. Reprinted by permission of the publisher.

FIRST EDITION

Library of Congress Cataloging-in-Publication Data

Palmer, Parker J.
    The active life: a spirituality of work, creativity, and caring /
Parker J. Palmer.—1st. ed.
        p.   cm.
    Includes bibliographical references.
    ISBN 0-06-066457-6
    1. Spirituality.   I. Title.
BV4501.2.P313   1990
248.8'8—dc20   89-45932
                                                                   CIP

90 91 92 93 94 HAD 10 9 8 7 6 5 4 3 2 1

This edition is printed on acid-free paper that meets the American National Standards Institute A39.48 Standards.

Contents

Preface

This book is about the activities that help to make us human —work, creativity, and caring—and I hope that the book itself bears evidence of them. Much work went into the writing, and much care. Whether the outcome is creative, others will have to say, but I know that the process of writing has been creative for me. It has helped renew my soul.

Many people have been integral to the creation of this book, whether they read the manuscript or not, and I want to thank them. They include Ed Beers, Sharon Craven, Susan Davis, Charlie Glasser, Robert W. Lynn, John Mogabgab, Henri Nouwen, Lewy Olfson, Max and LaVerne Palmer, Sally Palmer, Bob and Martha Rankin, Sharon Wallin, and Barbara Wheeler. I am grateful also to John Shopp, my editor, and to the Lilly Endowment, Inc., for support that helped this book along.

Six of the book's eight chapters revolve around stories and poems of the active life that I use in classes and retreats, and I want to thank the hundreds of people who have shared their lives and insights with me in those circles of teaching and learning. My teaching method is simple: I put one of these texts before the group, ask question after question about it, and as I listen the students become my teachers. There are many places in these pages where the voice of original insight belongs to one of these teacher-students. Because my memory fails me, I cannot give them the footnotes they deserve, but they have my gratitude for helping to make this book possible.

I am writing this preface at Las Palomas de Taos, an educational center in northern New Mexico. I arrived here on Good Friday and tomorrow is Easter. Looking out the windows above my writing table, I can see the Sangre de Cristo Mountains. Their peaks are deep in snow, their slopes covered with evergreens, the desert at their feet spiked and parched.

These images seem more than enough to me—images of winter and of spring, of aridity and of living water, of death and of life made new. They are more than enough to convey what my words in this book want to say—though the saying is less than the seeing, and the seeing is less than the being.

Las Palomas de Taos
Taos, New Mexico

The Active Life

1. Spirituality in Action: On Being Fully Alive

I. IMAGES OF SPIRITUAL LIFE

This book—this exploration of work, creativity, and caring in the world of action—is the result of my long journey toward the knowledge that I am not a monk.

My friends do not think that this is an especially deep insight, even if it did take me some years to reach it. After all, they remind me, I am not exactly silent, solitary, celibate, or orthodox, as a monk is supposed to be. I am the father of three, an activist in education and social change, a fellow traveler with the Quakers, a person of more extroversion and ego than a monk is meant to have. What made me think that I might be a monk of some sort, much less spend years learning that I am not? And what have I discovered about my calling to the active life in that process?

If those questions were only about me, I would not raise them here. But though my journey is unique in its details, the issues it has forced upon me are not mine alone.

Many people have been touched by the spiritual renaissance of the last thirty years, and that renaissance—from Thomas Merton onward—has been profoundly shaped by monastic metaphors and practices: silence, solitude, contemplation, centeredness. This spirituality, drawn from the richness of monastic tradition, offers a hope of peace to many people who must live in the harried world of action. Most of these people have never imagined moving to a monastery, but they would like to become more monklike, more contemplative, in the midst of their active lives.

Monastic spirituality has been a gift to many people, including me. But the fit between the monastic vision and life in the world of action is not always good. People who try to live by monastic norms sometimes fall so short ("I just can't find an hour a day to meditate") that they end up feeling guilty about leading "unspiritual" lives. People caught in the gap between monastic values and the demands of active life sometimes simply abandon the spiritual quest. And people who follow a spirituality that does not always respect the energies of action are sometimes led into passivity and withdrawal, into a diminishment of their own spirits.

In the spiritual literature of our time, it is not difficult to find the world of action portrayed as an arena of ego and power, while the world of contemplation is pictured as a realm of light and grace. I have often read, for example, that the treasure of "true self" can be found as we draw back from active life and enter into contemplative prayer. Less often have I read that this treasure can be found in our struggles to work, create, and care in the world of action.

Contemporary images of what it means to be spiritual tend to value the inward search over the outward act, silence over sound, solitude over interaction, centeredness and quietude and balance over engagement and animation and struggle. If one is called to monastic life, those images can be empowering. But if one is called to the world of action, the same images can disenfranchise the soul, for they tend to devalue the energies of active life rather than encourage us to move with those energies toward wholeness.

I want to share something of my journey among those images and realities because I know there are others walking a similar path.

II. JOURNEY OF A SOUL

I grew up in a Protestant family in a secular society and received a secular-Protestant education. I was prepared to take my place in the world of action, and I did—as citizen, parent, writer, teacher, administrator, community organizer. But somewhere along the line I began to fear that world, with its demands, its assaults on my sense of competence and self-worth, its threats of failure. As the meaning of my active life became more ambiguous, I embarked on a spiritual journey, a journey (as I saw it then) away from the world of action into the world of contemplation, away from the challenges of doing into the comforts of being. As a person who came to young adulthood in the sixties, I was supported in my quest by a counterculture whose slogans included "Don't just do something—stand there!"

Of course, I had to keep "doing" in order to stay alive, a task with many levels. So I was fortunate to find guidance far wiser than slogans in the writings of Thomas Merton. As a young man, Merton was filled with the energies of active life, and he lived them to the hilt, sometimes doing harm to himself and others. Fearing his own destructiveness, and guided (as he felt) by God toward spiritual discipline and celebration, Merton entered the Trappist monastery when he was nearly twenty-seven. He spent the next twenty-seven years exploring the monastic experience and metaphor in writings that have made a huge impact on the modern religious imagination. Largely because of Merton and his interpreters, the image of the monk has become a public counterweight to the gravitational pull of our activist age.

In my case, the image had such power that I not only thought about it and wrote about it but needed to act it out as well. Several years ago, I joined with seven other people, including two experienced monks, to develop a new form of monastic community that was to be ecumenical and open to men and women, whether celibate or not—a community not walled off from the world but still governed by monastic norms. Today that community continues. But after nearly three years, my share in it ended in the conclusion that I am not a monk but an activist.

I do not thrive on the monastic virtues of stability, centeredness, balance. As much as I may need those qualities in my life, the words do not name those moments when I feel most alive and most able to share life with others. I thrive on the vitality and variety of the world of action. I value spontaneity more than predictability, exuberance more than order, inner freedom more than the authority of tradition, the challenge of dialogue more than the guidance of a rule, eccentricity more than staying on dead center.

Of course, those pairs are not polar opposites, either/or choices. They are paradoxes, and I need to live in the creative tensions between their various poles. But the truth is that my activist soul is enlivened by moving closer to the pole that contemplative spirituality sometimes devalues or even denies. Perhaps my attempt to move the other way was driven less by a sense of vocation than by a fear of my own energies, by a desire to suppress them. Though I need to avoid the frenzy and violence that always lurk in the active life, I need even more to embrace my God-given powers and gifts. I need to fathom the spirit and truth of the active life.

As I reflect on the limits of monastic spirituality in my own life, I return to Thomas Merton not with a jaundiced eye but with renewed appreciation. It now seems to me that the remarkable thing about Merton was not only that he had the wisdom to choose monastic life as a containment against self-destruction, but that he had the heart to nurture his activist energies in an environment sometimes bent on suppressing them. The very qualities that weary activists have found so attractive in the monastic metaphor—such as silence, solitude, anonymity—were not Merton's primary traits. If they had been, we would not be discussing his life and thought. Merton retained activist energies and stayed deeply connected with the psyche of his age. Had he not, he would never have become an international influence in movements for justice and peace, and the mentor for a legion of seekers in the world of action.

From various biographies it is clear that Merton struggled

at great personal cost to maintain an activist spirit in the monastery. Not only did he often battle with authority; he battled too with a long string of physical ailments that may well have been brought on by the tensions in his life. I do not doubt Merton's contemplative calling. But perhaps Merton needed monasticism as a foil for his own development; perhaps he needed the tension between the monastic ethos and his own vitalities to help evoke his true self. If that is so, then some of us may find clues to a spirituality for active life not so much in Merton's rendering of monastic spirituality as in the tensions between Merton's spirit and the monastic life-form.

That, at least, is where I have learned most from my own encounter with monasticism—in the tensions. My sojourn with the monks brought me a fair share of personal discouragement and defeat. But those experiences were rich with clues that now help me understand the dynamics of the active life and the spirit of truth that such a life can contain. With gratitude for the monastic path and for those who walk it in health, I want to explore some other approaches to the issues of active life.

III. AN ANCIENT TUG-OF-WAR

A tug-of-war between active and contemplative life has gone on for a long time in the Western world. Though I am not an historian and my intent in this book is not scholarly analysis but personal understanding, a rough sense of this history may give us a better understanding of our own place in the life of action.[1]

In the ancient world, contemplation was valued more highly than action. For the ancients, the active life was merely a way of meeting material needs and maintaining a household, while contemplation offered a chance at transcendence, at union with the ideal or the divine. Plato's model person was the "philosopher king" who reigned over the model society—a society designed to support an elite whose primary ser-

vice would be thought and reflection. Jesus reflects this ancient bias in the story of Mary and Martha when he claims
that the reflective Mary has "chosen the better part," compared to her sister, who is immersed in the mundane tasks of
housework (Luke 10:42, JB). Rooted in this bias, the church
and the university became the preeminent institutions of
Western culture, in part because they harbored the life of
contemplation in a world where the active life was merely
what the masses did to survive.

But with the Age of Exploration and the Enlightenment,
with the rise of science, the Industrial Revolution, and urbanization, the rope was tugged the other way, and active life became more valued than contemplation. The reason for this
shift seems clear: With the tools of science and technology,
people are able to act for purposes far beyond mere sustenance
and survival. Now we can use the tools of action to change
the world, to invent our own reality, to make an historical
mark. Knowledge, once seen as an end in itself, becomes a
means to power. Action, not contemplation, becomes the
pathway to personal virtue, to social status, and even to "salvation" for many modern men and women.

Today, in some quarters of our society, there has been a
countermovement in this historic tug-of-war, a reaction to
the dominance of activist values: It is the spiritual renaissance
I spoke of earlier, the renewed search for contemplative values
in the flurry of our active lives. It is easy to understand why
this reaction set in and how inevitable it was. The active life
seems to have run amok in the twentieth-century West. Our
culture takes such overweening pride in the powers of action,
and is so filled with the desire to conquer and dominate everything in sight, that there is less and less health in us. For
those who see this sickness for what it is, recovery may seem
to lie in a return to contemplation.

But why continue the historic tug-of-war? Contemplation
and action ought not to be at war with one another, and as
long as they are, we will be at war within ourselves. There are

at least two ways toward a cessation of hostilities. One is to recognize that contemplation and action are not contradictions, but poles of a great paradox that can and must be held together. That paradox is the focus of chapter 2.

A second way to end the tug-of-war is simply to acknowledge that different people have different callings. If one is called to the active life, there is no more health to be found in dealing with the challenges of the monastery than Thomas Merton found in dealing with the challenges of the world of action. We must try to live responsively to both poles of the contemplative-active paradox. But we must honor the pole of our own calling, even as we stay open to the other, lest we lose our identity, our integrity, our well-being.

For people who are called to active life there are spiritualities that pose these very dangers. For example, there are versions of prayer that seem aimed at "keeping the lid on," at internalizing all the conflicts of one's life. But if the energies being contained involve one's truth, one's nature, then the lid is bound to blow. There are versions of our basic relation to God that seem aimed at bringing us under external authority rather than encouraging and educating the powers God has given us. When a person called to active life tries to submit to such guidance, diminishment and distortion can be the outcomes.

I know from my own life the damage that can be done by the energies that give rise to action, and I know the need for good guidance. But even as I grieve that damage, I deeply appreciate and respect those energies. To name them, I believe, is to name the living God—who has many names. I struggle with those parts of our spiritual tradition in which the energies of active life are more feared than revered, pictured as wild horses to be brought under control rather than life-giving streams that flow from the source. The feelings of diminishment and guilt that such spiritualities can engender may have some short-term role as prods to self-discovery. But they have no long-term place in the life of the spirit. People called to active life need to nurture a spirituality that does not fear the vitalities of action.

The core message of all the great spiritual traditions is "Be not afraid." Rather, be confident that life is good and trustworthy. In this light, the great failure is not that of leading a full and vital active life, with all the mistakes and suffering such a life will bring (along with its joys). Instead, the failure is to withdraw fearfully from the place to which one is called, to squander the most precious of all our birthrights—the experience of aliveness itself.

Joseph Campbell spoke of this birthright in words that I find compelling, if incomplete:

People say that what we're all seeking is a meaning for life. I don't think that's what we're really seeking. I think that what we are seeking is an experience of being alive, so that our life experiences on the purely physical plane will have resonances with our innermost being and reality, so that we actually feel the rapture of being alive. That's what it's finally all about. . . .[2]

I do not think that Campbell rejects the idea of meaning so much as he insists on the primacy of embodied, active experience as the way some of us will discover what it means to be alive. He implicitly criticizes spiritualities that withdraw from life in fear rather than risk the messiness of embodiment and action. Sometimes our quest for orderly meaning comes from fear of disorderly life, from our need to dampen the disrupting rapture of which Campbell speaks. We do just that when we heap layer upon layer of spiritual meaning on life's elemental forces, when we use theology or any other meaning-system to bury the incarnation.

For me, the heart of the spiritual quest is to know "the rapture of being alive," and (here is where I find Campbell incomplete) to allow that knowledge to transform us into celebrants, advocates, defenders of life wherever we find it. The experience of aliveness must never degenerate into a narcissistic celebration of self—for if it does, it dies. Aliveness is relational and communal, responsive to the reality and needs of others as well as to our own. For some of us, the primary path to that aliveness is called the active life. We need a spirituality which affirms and guides our efforts to act in ways that resonate with our innermost being and reality, ways that embody the vitalities God gave us at birth, ways that serve the great works of justice, peace, and love.

IV. ACTIVE LIFE AS BLESSING AND CURSE

The active life takes many forms, three of which are explored in this book—work, creativity, and caring. The three are not mutually exclusive and are often intertwined, but it will be helpful to name the main traits of each of them. By understanding each type of action, and how each differs from the others, we will be able to appreciate more about the range of issues raised by the active life.

Work is action driven by external necessity or demand. We work because we need to make a living, because we need to solve a problem, because we need to surmount or survive. I do not mean that we are mere robots when we work, totally determined by factors outside ourselves; we may choose whether to work, when to work, how to work. But work, as I use the word here, always involves the element of necessity, and that element leads to the characteristic dilemmas of this form of the active life.

Creativity, in contrast, is driven more by inner choice than by outer demand. An act cannot be creative if it is not born of freedom. In creative action, our desire is not to "solve" or "succeed" or "survive" but to give birth to something new; we want, for a while, to be less creaturely and more like the creator. If work reveals something of our bondage to the world, creativity reveals something of how we transcend it—and that fact gives rise to the dilemmas of creativity.

Caring is also action freely chosen. But in caring we aim not at giving birth to something new; we aim at nurturing, protecting, guiding, healing, or empowering something that already has life. The energy behind caring is compassion for others which, in turn, is energized by the knowledge that we are all in this together, that the fate of other beings has implications for our own fate. Caring may take a personal form, for instance, when we comfort a grieving friend. But it can also take form through movements for political and economic justice, in speaking on behalf of strangers whose oppression diminishes us all.

In the midst of these definitions we need to remember two things. First, these three forms of action are found together as well as apart (and together is how they often appear in this book). Work can be creative, creativity can be caring, and caring can be a quality of work.

Second, though these definitions may feel airy and abstract, remember that the active life is embodied life, everyday life—so ordinary we hardly notice it. We work in offices, farms, and homes. We act creatively in everything from gardening to raising children to writing a poem. We care by visiting a sick neighbor and by marching for peace. One way or another, most of us are involved in the active life day in and day out.

But for me, and for many people that I know, these ordinary activities contain an extraordinary mix of blessing and curse. The blessing is obvious, especially when we lose the chance or the capacity to do these ordinary things: the active life makes it possible for us to discover ourselves and our world, to test and extend our powers, to connect with other beings, to co-create a common reality. The joys of action are known to everyone who has done a job well, made something of beauty, given time and energy to a just cause. Take away the opportunity to work, to create, or to care—as our society does to too many people—and you have deprived someone of a chance to feel fully human.

But the active life also carries a curse. Many of us know what it is to live lives not of action but of frenzy, to go from day to day exhausted and unfulfilled by our attempts to work, create, and care. Many of us know the violence of active life, a violence we sometimes inflict on ourselves and sometimes inflict on our world. In action, we project our spirits outside ourselves. Sometimes we project shadows which do damage to others, and sometimes we project light that others want to extinguish. Action poses some of our deepest spiritual crises as well as some of our most heartfelt joys.

My aim in this book is to celebrate and criticize the active life, to explore its joys and pains, its problems and potentials, to understand the forces that both drive and deform our activity—but to do all this with reverence for the mystery of self-discovery and creation which is at the heart of human action. As I have pursued this aim, I have found less insight in theories and case studies than in stories and poems from various spiritual traditions that portray people in the midst of working, creating, and caring. Some people would find an analytic approach more helpful, but that is not the nature of this book (except for parts of this chapter and the next). This book is rooted primarily in fictional and mythical accounts of the active life that speak to me and, I hope, to some readers, for at least one reason: They represent the active life in the round and so offer us a chance to dwell in the subject in a complex, living, organic way—the way of imagination.

Barry Lopez speaks for me when he says that truth cannot "be reduced to aphorism or formula. It is something alive and unpronounceable. Story creates an atmosphere in which [truth] becomes discernible as pattern."[3] When truth is told through the imaginative patterns of stories and poems, we have a chance to be caught up and rewoven into truth's own designs. Though this book is about the quandaries of everyday life, it is not a "how to" book, and it offers no formulas or techniques for better living. But I believe that the stories and poems offer a far more practical thing: self-understanding that can illumine and help transform our lives.

The stories and poems that I use in this book come from diverse traditions: From ancient Chinese Taoism, from early biblical culture, from the Hasidic Judaism of eighteenth-century Europe, from one woman's struggle for justice in contemporary Latin America. I draw on such diverse sources for the same reason that I use stories and poems: To see truth in the round, we need many angles of vision, many voices of varied experience. We need, in the wonderful words of Douglas Steere, the benefits of "mutual irradiation" to appreciate the richness of active life.

I am sure that the angles afforded by my Taoist and Jewish texts are diminished by the fact that I read them through Christian eyes, to say nothing of the fact that I read the Christian texts through my own theological biases. I know, too, that everything I see and say is conditioned by the fact that I am white, male, middle-class, and North American. But these stories and poems have the strength to speak for themselves no matter what I say about them, and you will surely hear them speaking truths that I have yet to understand.

If story and truth are complex, the structure of this book is simple. It moves us through a sequence of central issues in the spirituality of active life.

- In chapter 2, I examine the nature of active life with special attention to its paradoxical partner, the life of contemplation, trying to show that the two are really one.
- In chapter 3, I explore the first of the six stories and poems on which the book is based. This one is a Taoist poem called "Active Life." It takes a critical look at the shadow side of action—our tendency toward knee-jerk reaction—and at the damage it does.
- Chapter 4 relates the Taoist tale of "The Woodcarver." This story is about a person working, creating, and caring in a way that confronts the shadow, moves through it, and offers us a model of what "right action" can be.
- With this model in mind, I turn to an Hasidic Jewish tale in chapter 5. This is the story of an angel who tries to relieve the world's suffering but ends up in failure and more

suffering. We will try to discover how this common experience relates to "right action."

- In chapter 6, I recall the biblical story of Jesus' entry into active life through his temptations in the desert. These are the same temptations that lead to the angel's failure and pain in chapter 5, but Jesus deals with them in a very different way.

- Chapter 7 explores another Jesus tale, the story of the feeding of five thousand people with a few loaves and fishes. Here we see the fruits of Jesus' struggle with the temptations of active life: He is able to act on the assumption of abundance, not scarcity, and by his action make abundance become a fact.

- In chapter 8, I share a poem by Julia Esquivel, a contemporary Guatemalan activist, who raises the question of scarcity and abundance in its ultimate form: Are our active lives oriented toward death or toward new life? Her challenge, her witness, reach to the heart of the life of action.

2. Action and Contemplation: A Living Paradox

I. TOWARD INTEGRATION

Our drive to aliveness expresses itself in two elemental and inseparable ways: action and contemplation. We may think of the two as contrary modes, but they are one at the source, and they seek the same end—to celebrate the gift of life. If we are to end the tug-of-war between them and understand their vital relatedness, we must abandon ordinary logic and embrace the insight of physicist Neils Bohr: "The opposite of a true statement is a false statement, but the opposite of a profound truth can be another profound truth."[1]

Rather than speak of contemplation and action, we might speak of contemplation-and-action, letting the hyphens suggest what our language obscures: that the one cannot exist without the other. When we fail to hold the paradox together, when we abandon the creative tension between the two, then both ends fly apart into madness. That is what often happens to contemplation-and-action in our culture of either/or. Action flies off into frenzy—a frantic and even violent effort to impose one's will on the world, or at least to survive against the odds. Contemplation flies off into escapism—a flight from the world into a realm of false bliss.

There is a scenario of three stages that may describe the movement that some of us make as we work out the relation of these paradoxical parts of our lives. It takes us from separation through alternation and sometimes to integration. Separation is the starting point for many of us, a stage in which we feel forced to make a choice between contemplative and active life. Because our culture tends to value action over contemplation, we often begin by choosing a life of activity that can become frantic, that exhausts and fragments our souls.

When exhaustion overcomes us, and we are too drained to keep up the pace, we move into the stage of alternation, which might be called the *vacation approach* to life. Exhausted by activity, we take a little vacation to refresh ourselves, then we plunge back into action until we are exhausted again, then we take another vacation until we renew the energy to wear ourselves down once more—and on the cycle goes.

Alternation is better than separation, but both stages reflect the mistaken notion that contemplation and action are mutually exclusive ways of life. By moving from separation to alternation we may save ourselves from terminal burnout, but we never allow the two poles of the paradox to interact in a way that would bring health to both ways of life. Our active lives remain harried and violent, never transformed by contemplation; our contemplative lives remain escapist, never transformed by action.

Many of us live a long time in the stage of alternation, but some people, at least some of the time, move on to the third stage, integration. This is the breakthrough into paradox, and we might be more likely to make it if we better understood how it happens. Some people make it simply because they are wise. But perhaps the breakthrough is most often made by people who abandon themselves so deeply to action that no vacation can help them. They become so profoundly exhausted that they are forced to give up all efforts to manage, direct, or control their lives. Compelled to live beyond ego and will-power, they find themselves falling into the sustaining power of paradox.

In the stage of integration we learn that contemplation-and-action are so intertwined that features we associate with one are always found at the heart of the other—just as the Chinese symbol of yang harbors a dark spot of yin, and the symbol of yin harbors a light spot of yang. Action becomes more than a matter of getting from here to there, but a contemplative affair as well, a path by which we may discover inner truth. Contemplation becomes more than a luxury to be indulged when the worries of the world are behind us, but a way of changing consciousness that may have more impact on the world than strategic action can have. Contemplation-and-action are integrated at the root, and their root is in our ceaseless drive to be fully alive.

To be fully alive is to act. The capacity to act is the most obvious difference between the quick and the dead. But action is more than movement; it is movement that involves expression, discovery, re-formation of ourselves and our world. *I understand action to be any way that we can co-create reality with other beings and with the Spirit.* Through action we both express and learn something of who we are, of the kind of world we have or want. Action, like a sacrament, is the visible form of an invisible spirit, an outward manifestation of an inward power. But as we act, we not only express what is in us and help give shape to the world; we also receive what is outside us, and we reshape our inner selves. When we act, the world acts back, and we and the world are co-created.

To be fully alive is to contemplate. By contemplation I do not mean the practice of a particular technique, like sitting in the lotus position and chanting a mantra. In fact, the obsession with contemplative technique seems to me to reflect the hubris of technology more than the humility of the Spirit. *I understand contemplation to be any way that we can unveil the illusions that masquerade as reality and reveal the reality behind the masks.* One of the great threats to full aliveness is the sleight of hand practiced by our egos and our culture to keep us from seeing things as they are. Contemplation happens any time that we catch the magician deceiving us and we get a glimpse of the truth behind the trick. Whether it is a happy truth or a hard one, that truth will always quicken our lives.

With these definitions it is easy to see that contemplation-and-action are not apart from each other but are parts of each other. Whenever we act in a way that penetrates illusion and brings us closer to reality, that action is contemplative. I think, for example, of John Howard Griffin, a white man who, in the mid-fifties, darkened his skin with chemicals and traveled as a black man in the South.[2] In that risky action he pierced the illusion of equality in America and touched the reality of racism—and he touched it more palpably than some of us do in prayer.

By the same token, contemplation can become a form of action, a movement of expression, discovery, re-creation. I think, for example, of Merton, the monk who spent most of the fifties sitting and praying in a cloister in rural Kentucky. Late in that decade he began to write of a great racial conflict that would shatter American life, a prophecy that one prominent urban activist attacked for its patent arrogance: "How dare this escapist monk tell those of us who labor for justice in the cities that our work will fail?" Several years later that critic publicly apologized to Merton, acknowledging that the monk's contemplative eye saw into racism more deeply than the eye of the activist.[3] Despite the fact that Merton never marched in a demonstration or participated in formal politics, his contemplation had an impact on the history of our century.

Of course, few of us have acted as dramatically as John Howard Griffin or plunged as deeply into contemplation as Thomas Merton. But that is beside the point. Rightly understood, contemplation and action are standard features of ordinary, everyday life. Our contemplative action may be raising a child, making things with wood, delivering mail, managing a company, operating a computer, volunteering to feed the hungry, writing a book. Our active contemplation may involve staring out a window, reading a book, thinking long and hard, grieving a painful loss. Whatever our action, it can express and help shape our souls and our world. Whatever our contemplation, it can help us see the reality behind the veils. Contemplation and action are not high skills or specialties for the virtuoso few. They are the warp and weft of human life, the interwoven threads that form the fabric of who we are and who we are becoming.

When we take that fabric apart to examine it, we risk destroying something of beauty that we will never be able to reweave. But since most of this book will display the whole fabric of contemplation-and-action through stories and poems, I need to look separately at the two threads in this chapter. So many misconceptions surround these two words, and so many obstructions surround our living of them, that it is important to examine them individually here. I want to approach that examination not as someone unraveling a tapestry but as a weaver preparing to sit at the loom to weave—and to be woven.

II. THE NATURE OF ACTION

If you are unemployed, if you are forced to do work that brings neither enough money or recognition, if you are young and uncertain about where you are going, or if you are unhappily retired, one of the most painful questions anyone can ask you may be simply "What do you do?" If you are unprepared, if you have not reflected on your situation and found ground to stand on, that simple question can open a dangerous chasm beneath your feet and trigger fierce defenses. Why so?

One explanation is that most of us need jobs to stay afloat financially, so when we cannot say what we do, the pit of financial instability opens beneath us. But that does not explain why the chasm may also open up for people who have no real economic concerns. Why do some people who work at home while their spouses are out making an ample income still experience vertigo when the question is asked?

Another explanation is that we are social beings who need to have meaningful places in the work of the world. Few people want to be marginal to society, and the way one moves toward the center is to have work that brings income or prestige. But this explanation also leaves questions unanswered. Why do some people who have retired from positions of power and visibility, people who have nothing left to prove, still sense the void when their "active days" are over, still need to justify themselves by rehearsing their achievements? Or, to turn it around, why do some dispossessed people who have no chance at the center of the circle live with more zest than many who are wealthy and well-connected?

Perhaps the primitive fear that some of us feel when we cannot answer the question "What do you do?" comes from a deep, unconscious intuition that inaction is a sign of death. When we are not "doing" we are forcibly reminded of our own mortality; we experience a sort of dying through inactivity. But when we are acting we can say to the world and to ourselves that we are here, we are alive, we are making a difference. Indeed, by acting we imagine that we can leave something of ourselves behind, marks that might give us a kind of immortality. In raising a child or shaping an institution or writing a book we may carry the silent hope that our mortal lives can somehow defy the barriers of death.

At this point, we often hear a voice of conventional wisdom. it warns us of the ego, the pride, the foolishness involved in trying to cheat death through action. We need to accept death, the voice tells us, accept the limits of our lives, or we will spend our energies building houses of cards. No matter how we exert ourselves to reach for immortality, death will sweep all our works away.

There is wisdom in that counsel, but there is danger too—the danger of a passivity that retards the development of the self and the world, a dying before we are dead. Dylan Thomas spoke a corrective word when he said, "Do not go gentle into that good night."[4] Without deluding ourselves about achieving immortality, we need to act freely and sometimes boldly to express ourselves in ways that offer our gifts to others. Everyone has the right, perhaps even the imperative, to reach for self-expression not to gratify every whim but to serve as one was created to serve. Action, even death-defying action, is one way to claim that right. It is sad to see people whose actions are driven by foolish dreams of grandeur. But it is even sadder to see people who have forfeited, or been denied, the chance to act with strength—people painfully lacking in the sense of self that comes as we declare and discover our own truth through the active life.

Much human action is laced with the problem of pride, the pride that shows itself when we try to impose our ego-designs on a child or a co-worker or a project. Not only is our action sometimes fueled by an inflated ego; action can lead to further inflation of the ego as well. But the development of a healthy ego is essential to personal and corporate health. Action—even action entangled with egotism—is a major source of that development.

Prideful action is often followed by a fall. But we make a mistake when we try to avoid that fall by withdrawing from action. When we suffer the cycle of inflation and deflation, we learn that it is one of the great engines of the human journey, one of the great mentors of the human spirit. I treasure that early Christian theologian who railed against the notion that the "fall" of Adam and Eve was pure and simple sin. Instead, he called it *felix culpa,* the happy sin, since without it we would still be living in the boredom of dreaming innocence and the great adventure of human history would never have gotten underway.[5]

The fall gave us the "gifts" of doubt, ambiguity, alienation. These do not feel like gifts when we first experience them. To know them as the gifts they are, we must enter into the struggles they pose for us. Once inside, we have a chance to find the self that remains hidden when we feel confident and secure, the seeking self that draws us into the human adventure. And that self is one of the greatest gifts we have.

To put all of this into a single word, action is *risky.* When we draw back from action, we are often motivated not by humility but by fear of risk. We risk so many things when we act: taking a fall, failing to achieve a goal, appearing incompetent, evoking criticism or competition or resistance or anger, or simply being ignored. But most of all, we risk exposing ourselves—selves at once strong and fragile, known and unknown—to the scrutiny of the world and, sometimes less mercifully, to the scrutiny of ourselves.

The greatest risk in action is the risk of self-revelation, and that is also action's greatest joy. No one can know us fully, not even we ourselves, but when we act, something of our inner mystery often emerges, and it can shock or delight when it does. In this age of the machine, we seem to imagine human action as a safe and predictable play-out of instructions stored in the mind, something like the functioning of a word processor. But real action is not simply the manifestation of the mind's concept or design. Real action is part mind itself, as well as spirit and soul.

When I act, as poet Theodore Roethke says, "I learn by going where I have to go."[6] Or, as the more popular saying has it, "How can I know what I think until I hear myself say it?" I am having that experience right now, as I write. Each new sentence is an unfolding of ideas and images that I did not know I had within me until I brought them up and out in the act of writing. And that entails risk.

Action has a life of its own, related to what we think we are doing, but often full of surprises. Action can take courses and have consequences that are decidedly independent of our own designs for it. For example, our actions sometimes reveal something false in us; as I write, my own words occasionally judge me. Or, our actions may reveal something true in us that others want to censure, as when our inner guidance defies conventional order. And sometimes our acts can change the course of our lives in ways quite beyond anticipation, as when we allow ourselves to care deeply for a person or a cause. The question is whether we are willing to act in the face of these risks, willing to learn and grow from whatever new truths our actions may reveal.

There is an intimate link between our capacity for risk-taking and our commitment to learning and growing. A risk is an effort that may not succeed, and the bigger the risk, the less the chance of success. So why would anyone take such risks? There are many reasons, but one of the most creative is that by risking we may learn more about ourselves and our world, and the bigger the risk, the greater the learning. If we do not value learning, we will not risk, and our actions will be limited to small and predictable arenas in which we know we can succeed.

Our capacity to take risks and learn from them depends heavily on whether we understand action as *instrumental* or *expressive*. The instrumental image, which dominates Western culture, portrays action as a means to predetermined ends, as an instrument or tool of our intentions. The only possible measure of such action is whether it achieves the ends at which it is aimed. Instrumental action is governed by the logic of success and failure; it discourages us from risk-taking because it values success over learning, and it abhors failure whether we learn from it or not.

Instrumental action always wants to win, but win or lose, it inhibits our learning. If we win we think we know it all and have nothing more to learn. If we lose we feel so defeated that learning is a hollow consolation. Instrumental action traps us in a system of praise or blame, credit or shame, a system that gives primacy to goals and external evaluations, devalues the gift of self-knowledge, and diminishes our capacity to take the risks that may yield growth.

I find it fascinating that the most "successful" of all modern activities—science—is one that rejects success and failure as the primary norms for its acts. For the pure scientist, a failed experiment is no failure at all, but a vital step toward learning the truth. Such "failure" narrows the range of relevant hypotheses to be tested and may contribute some positive findings as well. Science, seen by many as our most powerful instrumentality, has achieved its eminence in part by freeing itself from the stranglehold of instrumentalism.

Of course, scientific knowledge is often used by technology in action of the most instrumental sorts. Such action, action that links means to ends, will always be a part of our lives, will always play a central role in a world with finite resources and infinite needs. As long as we live embodied lives, the demands of instrumental action will always be with us.

But when the standards of instrumentalism dominate, our action is impoverished and our lives are diminished. Only when we act *expressively* do we move toward full aliveness and authentic power. An expressive act is one that I take not to achieve a goal outside myself but to express a conviction, a leading, a truth that is within me. An expressive act is one taken because if I did not take it I would be denying my own insight, gift, nature. By taking an expressive act, an act not obsessed with outcomes, I come closer to making the contribution that is mine to make in the scheme of things.

The doing of pure science is an expressive act, an act that simply manifests the scientist's own desire to know the truth. Paradoxically, as science demonstrates, an expressive act is more likely to achieve real ends than is an instrumental act calculated to reach such ends but not rooted in the actor's own reality. When an act is true to one's nature it is more likely to have outcomes that are true to the field of action. I do not mean that we will always find the outcomes of expressive action to be acceptable, pleasing, or "good." I mean simply that whatever the outcomes may be, they will be convergent with a larger sustaining truth. They will not be temporary illusions imposed on reality by our false and frail images of how things ought to be.

And that brings us to the subject of contemplation and to the difficult insight at the heart of contemplative life: Truth is always preferable to illusion, no matter how closely the illusion conforms to our notion of the good—or how far the truth diverges from it.

III. THE NATURE OF CONTEMPLATION

When we reflect on the nature of action, we inevitably come to the question "What is real?" Every action originates in some assessment of reality, no matter how mistaken. No action will have lasting effects if it is inconsistent with reality. Ultimately, action will help to reveal what the reality is, if we pay attention to its outcomes. These are the crucial links between action and contemplation, for the function of contemplation in all its forms is to penetrate illusion and help us to touch reality.

Contemplation is difficult for many of us because we have invested so much in illusion. Sometimes we even seem wedded to illusion as a way of survival. When I look at my own life I am appalled at the illusions I have cultivated simply to get me through the day—illusions about my motives, my abilities, my desires. I am appalled at the pain that my illusions have caused me and others, and at the thought that right now I harbor illusions I cannot even name because I depend on the belief that they are real.

When I look at the society around me, I see illusions as thick as my own: the illusion that violence solves problems, that both rich and poor deserve their fate, that young people sent to die in wars fought to defend the rich are heroes rather than victims, that murderous drugs are the way beyond despair—just to name a few.

These illusions serve a societal function: They keep us in place. If my child is murdered in a distant war for wealth, the government awards medals, and I display them to keep from going mad. If my life is degraded by racism and injustice, the economy dispenses cocaine to dull my anger, and soon I can feel nothing at all. Meanwhile, the people who benefit most from the illusions are declaring "peace in our time" and "a war on drugs," more illusions, but so functional for both perpetrators and victims that they are widely mistaken for reality.

This is why the contemplative moment, the moment when illusion is stripped away and reality is revealed, is so hard to come by; there is a vast conspiracy against it. But the hopeful fact is that all of us have such moments whether or not we seek them, are ready for them, or know what to do when they arrive. Try as I might, I have found little help in the intentional disciplines of contemplation, so I have no spiritual techniques to suggest here. But I have learned that life compensates for my disability by providing moments of unintentional contemplation, and those are the experiences that I want to explore. If we pay attention to them, such experiences can become the disciplines of contemplation for some of us.

In the moments I am thinking of, the foundations of life often seem swept away, so we may find it difficult to experience them as either contemplative or hopeful, especially if we labor under another common illusion, one that pictures contemplation as a direct flight to Nirvana. But if we drop this notion of how contemplation is supposed to feel, we begin to see that life makes contemplatives of all of us, whether we want to be contemplatives or not. The only question is whether we can name and claim those moments of opportunity for what they are.

For example, there is the experience we commonly call *disillusionment,* when a trusted friend lets us down, an institution we had relied on fails us, a vision we had believed in turns out to be a hoax, or—worst of all—when we discover ourselves to be less than we had thought. Many of us try hard to avoid such experiences, and when we are in the midst of them we go through a kind of dying. But the very name we give these moments tells us that something positive is happening through our pain. We say we are being "dis-illusioned." That is, we are being stripped of some illusions about life, about others, about ourselves. As our illusions are removed, like barriers on a road, we have a chance to take that road farther toward truth. Instead of commiserating and offering a shoulder to cry on when a friend says that he or she is disillusioned, we ought to congratulate, celebrate, and ask the friend how we can help the process go deeper still.

Pain is one of the sure signs that contemplation is happening. Contemplation may lead eventually to bliss, but first it will give us the pain of knowing that some of our dearest convictions are shallow, inadequate, wrong. Contemplation first deprives us of familiar comforts. Then it replaces them with an inner emptiness in which new truth, often alien and unsettling truth, can emerge. The contemplative journey from illusion to reality may have peace as its destination, but en route it usually passes through some fearsome places.

If disillusionment is one of life's natural forms of contemplation, the experience of *dislocation* is another. This happens when we are forced by circumstance to occupy a very different standpoint from our normal one, and our angle of vision suddenly changes to reveal a strange and threatening landscape. I think, for example, of the man who lives forty years in perfect health until one day the doctor tells him he has terminal cancer. I think of the woman who has held the same job for thirty years until an overnight corporate takeover leaves her unemployed at age fifty-eight. I think of the person finally forced to admit that alcohol has made life so unbearable that the only choice is to change or to die.

The value of dislocation, like the value of disillusionment, is in the way that it moves us beyond illusion, so we can see reality in the round—since what we are able to see depends entirely on where we stand. Standing in the middle of a field, it is easy to imagine that the earth is flat. Standing on the moon and looking back at our planet, we can see more clearly what her true form is.

Of course, contemplation that comes through dislocation is likely to leave us lonely; others often do not share our dislocated view of things, and sometimes they are threatened by our new truth. I once heard the story of a medieval Irish monk who died and was buried, as was the custom, in the monastery wall. One day the monks heard noises from within the wall and removed the stones to find their brother alive and well. He began to tell them what he had learned on his journey beyond—and everything he said was contrary to the teachings of the church. So the brothers put him back in the wall and sealed the crypt forever.

That story suggests one more way that life draws us into accidental contemplation, the way of *unbidden solitude.* Some of us find it as hard to choose solitude as to choose dislocation or disillusionment because solitude removes us from the collective life that often reinforces our comforting illusions. But life sends many moments when the group excludes us willy-nilly, moments when we say or feel or do something that the group does not want to deal with, moments when we are forced to find our way without collective support. In these moments, we once again have the chance to penetrate illusion and touch reality.

Solitude is a painful condition at first, as are disillusionment and dislocation. But, unlike those two, solitude is something that sometimes grows on people. There is a reason for this. Disillusionment and dislocation are temporary conditions, passages we must make in order to move beyond illusion and live in truth. But involuntary solitude is the permanent truth of our lives: We are born in solitude, we die in solitude, and we have opportunities to learn to live creatively with that fact in the years between birth and death. The fruit of disillusionment and dislocation is the capacity to enter and enjoy our solitude, compelled by the painful grace of a life process that is bent on helping us to "get real."

Solitude is not simply physical isolation. It is easy to be alone and yet continue to be in the crowd, to be governed by collective values; and it is possible to be physically in the midst of a crowd and yet to be in solitude. To be in solitude means to be in possession of my heart, my identity, my integrity. It means to refuse to let my life and my meanings be dictated by other people or by an impersonal culture. To be in solitude is to claim my birthright of aliveness on its own terms, terms that respect the life around me but do not demean my own. The solitary is someone who, to paraphrase Merton, is able to give her heart away because it is in her possession to give—a possession not possible when we are caught in the silent conspiracy of collective illusions.

So solitude is not antithetical to community. The poet Rilke once defined love as the capacity of two solitudes to "protect and border and greet each other," and that kind of love is the key to the paradoxical relationship of solitude and community.[7] The healthy community is one that leaves the solitude, the integrity, of each individual intact; if its members do not respect their own solitude, they will continually violate the solitude of others. The only thing we have to bring to community is ourselves, so the contemplative process of recovering our true selves in solitude is never selfish. It is ultimately the best gift we can give to others.

IV. THE HIDDEN WHOLENESS

If we are to understand the paradox of contemplation-and-action, we must attend to what Thomas Merton called "the hidden wholeness" that lies beneath the broken surface of our lives.[8] Until we know the hidden wholeness we will live in a world of dualisms, of forced but false choices between being and doing that result in action that is mere frenzy or in contemplation that is mere escape.

Our movement toward the hidden wholeness is not easily mapped because it is different for each person and always a mystery. But I can at least suggest the general direction of that movement, which is downward—contrary to the upward imagery of much Western spirituality with its fear of "the fall." Annie Dillard has offered some words about downwardness, and about the hidden wholeness toward which it takes us, that are full of insight for our exploration into contemplation-and-action:

In the deeps are the violence and terror of which psychology has warned us. But if you ride these monsters deeper down, if you drop with them farther over the world's rim, you find what our sciences cannot locate or name, the substrate, the ocean or matrix or ether which buoys the rest, which gives goodness its power for good, and evil its power for evil, the unified field: our complex and inexplicable caring for one another, and for our life together here. This is given. It is not learned.[9]

With Merton, Dillard knows that there is unity behind diversity, a wholeness behind the divergent forces of life. We find this wholeness, she says, not in an upward sweep to abstraction but in a downward plunge to the depths. This image of the spiritual quest is challenging, even frightening, in a culture that seeks wholeness in atmospheric generalities rather than in subterranean stuff. But I believe that the culture is wrong and that Dillard is right. We will find the hidden wholeness on which contemplation-and-action depends only if we are willing to go down and into our lives, not up and out of them as we are sometimes urged to do.

Dillard also departs from convention by insisting that the hidden substrate of our lives does not conform to normal standards of goodness. It "gives goodness its power for good," but it also gives "evil its power for evil." Here is an even more challenging, more frightening, notion in a culture that puts good and evil in airtight compartments, picturing them as antithetical impulses.

Again, I believe Dillard is wiser than the culture. When we plumb the depths of full aliveness, we draw close to the source that empowers all else, and in that power there is not only grace but danger, not only healing but wounding, not only life but death. Dillard is saying neither more nor less than the prophet Isaiah: "I am Yahweh, unrivaled, I form the light and create the dark. I make good fortune and create calamity, it is I, Yahweh, who do all this" (Isa. 45:7, JB). When we meet the Spirit that gives life we encounter *all* the powers, including death, and we cannot be selective.

In fact, if Dillard is right, the clue to full aliveness is found in the very forces of calamity that we would avoid if we had the power to choose. Speaking of the "monsters" we will meet on our journey downward, she urges us to "ride these monsters deeper down." Once more she upsets the conventional wisdom that warns us to flee from monsters lest we lose our lives. On the contrary, Dillard suggests, those monsters are the only reliable guides to the deeper reaches of our lives. Only by riding them down, despite the risks, will we be able to find the primal source of ourselves and our world.

Doing so, of course, requires a radical change of perspective for many of us. We must abandon the commonsense notion that the monsters we meet within ourselves are enemies to be destroyed. Instead, we must cultivate the hope that they can become companions to be embraced, guides to be followed, albeit with caution and respect. For only our monsters know the way down to that inner place of unity and wholeness; only these creatures of the night know how to travel where there is no light.

Though this change of perspective is radical, it contains a common sense of its own. The nonmonstrous parts of ourselves, the parts we consider angelic, are parts that separate us from others; they make for distinction, not unity. These parts give us pride because they make us different, not because they unite us with the common lot of humankind. Our successes and our glories are not the stuff of community, but our sins and our failures are. In those difficult areas of our lives we confront the human condition, and we begin to learn compassion for all beings who share the limits of life itself. It is not the angels in us but the fallen angels who know the way down, down to the hidden wholeness.

For example, if I allow my life to be deformed by the fallen angel called "fear of failure," I will never be fully alive. I will withhold myself from actions that might fail, or ignore evidence of failure when it happens. But if I could ride that fear all the way down, I might break out of my self-imposed isolation and become connected with many other lives, because failure and the fear of it is universal. I would learn that failure is a natural fact, a way of discerning what to try next. I would be empowered to take more risks, which means to embrace more life, and in the process I would become more connected with others. The monster called fear of failure (or ridicule, or criticism, or foolishness, or any of the other fears that are so easy to regard as mortal enemies) would become a demanding but empowering guide toward relatedness.

But on *this* side of such an experience, we may wonder why we should go anywhere near the monsters, let alone ride them all the way down. After all, they are monsters, and they do harbor powers of destruction as well as of creativity. Even if riding the monsters is the only way to reach safe ground, there is no guarantee that we will get there. People have fallen off before the end of the journey and have been stranded in some bad places. So why take the risk of riding the monsters in the first place?

My own experience offers a small parable to answer that question. It happened several years ago in the outdoor challenge program called Outward Bound. I took the course in my early forties, a time of life when monsters abound, and in the middle of that course I was asked to confront the thing I had feared most since I had first heard about Outward Bound: A gossamer strand was hooked to a harness around my body, I was backed up to the top of a 110-foot cliff, and I was told to lean out over God's own emptiness and walk down the face of that cliff to the ground eleven stories below.

I remember the cliff too well. It started with a five-foot drop to a small ledge, then a ten-foot drop to another ledge, then a third and final drop all the way down. I tried to negotiate the first drop; my feet instantly went out from under me, and I fell heavily to the first ledge. "I don't think you quite have it yet," the instructor observed astutely. "You are leaning too close to the rock face. You need to lean much farther back so your feet will grip the wall."

That advice, like the advice of some spiritual traditions, went against my every instinct. Surely one should hug the wall, not lean out over the void! But on the second drop I tried to lean back; better, but not far enough, and I hit the second ledge with a thud not unlike the first. "You still don't have it," said the ever-observant instructor. "Try again."

Since my next try would be the last one, her counsel was not especially comforting. But try I did, and much to my amazement I found myself moving slowly down the rock wall. Step-by-step I made my way with growing confidence until, about halfway down, I suddenly realized that I was heading toward a very large hole in the rock, and—not knowing anything better to do—I froze. The instructor waited a small eternity for me to thaw out, and when she realized that I was showing no signs of life she yelled up, "Is anything wrong, Parker?" as if she needed to ask. To this day I do not know the source of the childlike voice that came up from within me, but my response is a matter of public record: "I don't want to talk about it."

The instructor yelled back, "Then I think it's time you learned the Outward Bound motto." Wonderful, I thought. I am about to die, and she is feeding me bromides. But then she spoke words I have never forgotten, words so true that they empowered me to negotiate the rest of that cliff without incident: "If you can't get out of it, get into it." Bone-deep I knew that there was no way out of this situation except to go deeper into it, and with that knowledge my feet began to move.

That is why we must sometimes ride the monsters all the way down. Some monsters simply will not go away. They are too big to walk around, too powerful to overcome, too clever to outsmart. The only way to deal with them is to move toward them, with them, into them, through them. We must learn to befriend some of these primitive powers that seem so much like enemies. In the process we will find them working for us, not against us, working for life, not for death.

When we live a full life of contemplation-and-action, the monsters will always be aroused, and we will be compelled to search the depths. It is good to know that those very monsters can take us to the depths we need to explore. It is even better to know that in those depths we can find the hidden wholeness that unites and energizes us, the source and the power that make us fully alive.

3. "Active Life": The Shadow Side

I. AN IRONIC CRITIQUE

Beginning with this chapter, and throughout the rest of the book, our exploration of the active life will be made by means of stories and poems. So I want to say a few more words about learning from fictions and myths.

Some readers may doubt that insight into the factual world of action can come through fictional texts. Perhaps they will find the words of Eli Wiesel as challenging as I have: "Some events do take place but are not true; others are although they never occurred."[1] The tales that I explore in this book sometimes defy fact and logic, but when they do, it is for the sake of truth. Truth is a complex network of relationships, and we are drawn into it through the complex patterns of stories and poems. By exploring mythical accounts of action that are truthful in ways that mere facts never can be, we gain formative images and metaphors with which to criticize and celebrate our active lives.

More than that, we gain new friends. I have lived with these tales for some years, and the gifts they have given me go far beyond images and insights. They have given me companions who are sometimes more vivid than real people, guides who can be called on at moments when I need their help. I hope that the reader will form new friendships, as well as new ideas, in the course of this book. The beings who inhabit these stories and poems can goad us and guide us with their living presence long after our abstract ideas about them have faded from mind.

A comment by Martin Buber about the power of stories says all that I am trying to say:

A story must be told in such a way that it constitutes help in itself. My grandfather was lame. Once they asked him to tell a story about his teacher. And he related how his teacher used to hop and dance while he prayed. My grandfather rose as he spoke, and he was so swept away by his story that he began to hop and dance to show how the master had done. From that hour he was cured of his lameness. That's how to tell a story.[2]

In this chapter and the next, I reflect on two prose poems from Chuang Tzu, a fourth-century B.C. Chinese Taoist teacher. The translations were done by Thomas Merton (with the help of Chinese scholar John C. H. Wu), and while the texts are said to be faithful to the original language they are also filtered through Merton's sensibilities as a twentieth-century person.

Merton wrote over fifty books, and when he weighed his own work toward the end of his life, *The Way of Chuang Tzu* came up as one of his clear favorites.[3] One reason is obvious: Chuang Tzu is a charming, rascally character with a keen eye for human foibles and a splendid sense of humor, who delights in upsetting apple carts, but does it all with a transparent love for humanity. Since that description fits Merton himself, it is easy to see why he was drawn to the Taoist sage.

But there is a deeper reason for Merton's affinity with Chuang Tzu, I think. Merton the Christian found insight in the apparently alien tradition of Taoism, insight that did not compete with Christianity but sometimes completed it. Perhaps some symbols and formulas of Christian theology had grown old for Merton, and he found in Chuang Tzu the same freshness of imagery that the parables of Jesus must have had for their original hearers. In the kind of teaching that Jesus and Chuang Tzu did, freshness is crucial; the teaching counts on taking you by surprise, and once the images become pre-

dictable they stop teaching altogether. That two such different characters as Chuang Tzu and Jesus, coming from two
such different cultures, could end up teaching convergent
truths in similar ways is further evidence of the wholeness
that is hidden behind the world's diversities.

With this brief background, let us see what Chuang Tzu
has to say about the life of action:

"Active Life"*

If an expert does not have some problem to vex him,
   he is unhappy!
If a philosopher's teaching is never attacked, she pines
   away!
If critics have no one on whom to exercise their spite,
   they are unhappy.
All such people are prisoners in the world of objects.

He who wants followers, seeks political power.
She who wants reputation, holds an office.
The strong man looks for weights to lift.
The brave woman looks for an emergency in which she
   can show bravery.
The swordsman wants a battle in which he can swing
   his sword.
People past their prime prefer a dignified retirement,
   in which they may seem profound.
People experienced in law seek difficult cases to extend
   the application of laws.
Liturgists and musicians like festivals in which they
   parade their ceremonious talents.
The benevolent, the dutiful, are always looking for
   chances to display virtue.

---

*Because inclusive language is important to me, I have altered this poem, whose
original references are all male, by using some female and some gender-neutral
references. Wherever possible, I have done this with other poems and stories, as
noted. I have not made such alterations when it seemed to me that the text was
attempting to portray the so-called masculine dimension of both men and
women.

Where would the gardener be if there were no more
    weeds?
What would become of business without a market of
    fools?
Where would the masses be if there were no pretext
    for getting jammed together and making noise?
What would become of labor if there were no superfluous objects to
    be made?

Produce! Get results! Make money! Make friends!
   Make changes!
Or you will die of despair!

Those who are caught in the machinery of power take no joy except
in activity and change—the whirring of the machine! Whenever an
occasion for action presents itself, they are compelled to act; they
cannot help themselves. They are inexorably moved, like the machine of which they are a part. Prisoners in the world of objects,
they have no choice but to submit to the demands of matter! They
are pressed down and crushed by external forces, fashion, the market, events, public opinion. Never in a whole lifetime do they recover their right mind! The active life! What a pity![4]

    Before you dismiss Chuang Tzu as a total cynic about the
active lives that many of us must lead, you need to know that
irony is one of his chief teaching tools. He caricatures our activity in order to draw attention to features we would rather
overlook. Though his sketch does not do justice to all that we
are, it forces us to examine our action, its motives and outcomes, with our blinders off. As his other poems make clear
(including the one I use in the next chapter), Chuang Tzu re-
gards certain forms of the active life as vital and authentic.
But here he mocks a version of the active life that is all too
common among us, and we need to understand his critique if
we are to come to terms with ourselves.
    Although this poem was written in the fourth century B.C.,
its references and mood seem amazingly modern. No doubt
this is partly due to Merton taking license as a translator so
that the poem would speak to modern men and women. But

other translations I have seen have much the same contemporary tone, which suggests a more significant conclusion: The problem of action is not as modern as we think. So often we excuse our frenzy by attributing it to such twentieth-century ills as urbanization, technology, mass society, and rapid social change—an analysis that locates the problem, and therefore the solution, outside ourselves. But, if Chuang Tzu was protesting the pathologies of action over two millennia ago, there is no reason to believe that even a radical change in social circumstances would return us to sanity. Apparently, we have long carried the problem of action with us, and so the solutions are likely to be with us as well.

II. ON ACTION, REACTION, AND THE PROFESSIONS

Chuang Tzu's critique of the active life in this poem is simple: Too much of our action is really *re*action. Such "doing" does not flow from free and independent hearts, he says, but depends on external provocation. It does not come from our sense of who we are and what we want to do, but from our anxious reading of how others define us and of what the world demands. When we react this way we do not act humanly; we become cogs in a machine whose every move is forced by what is happening elsewhere in the interlocked system of cogs. "All such people are prisoners in the world of objects."

This is not a happy picture, but there is truth in it. Too many of us consent, or are forced, to spend time doing things for which we have no heartfelt reason. If we were asked, "Why are you doing this?" we would not know how to answer. Somehow a situation emerged in which "this" had to be done, and somehow we ended up doing it. We do it to hold a job, to make a living, to satisfy the expectations of others, to fill our time, to evade the fact that we don't know what else to do—but not because the doing comes from inside us. When our action is dictated by factors external to our souls, we do not live active lives but reactive lives.

History, daily experience, and the nightly news offer endless examples, from the political to the personal, of the inexorable logic of reaction. One nation angers another nation, the harsh rhetoric of ideology is aimed across borders, and soon weapons are aimed and fired as well. Rich topsoil is depleted by constant plowing and planting because short-term economics "demand" it, despite the irreplaceable long-term losses. One driver angers another on the street, hard words are exchanged, a gun is drawn from the glove compartment, and someone is murdered. A welfare clerk curtly dismisses a mother in desperate circumstances because her case falls just outside the guidelines.

Ironically, in cases such as these, the actors often claim that they acted to exercise or protect their freedom, even as the knee-jerk nature of their responses proves that they have lost the freedom to act. If they were acting rather than reacting, they would transcend the tight, deterministic logic of their situations. They would escape the reflex response and claim the freedom of authentic action.

But Chuang Tzu goes beyond the claim that our action is too often reaction. His deeper criticism is that many of us intentionally seek out those situations that will trigger our favored reactions: "The strong man looks for weights to lift. The brave woman looks for an emergency in which she can show bravery." And, we might add, the nation or person with weapons looks for a chance to use them, the corporation that owns farmland looks for a chance to exploit it, the clerk with rules in hand looks for someone to exclude. Chuang Tzu is describing the actor as addict, totally dependent on situations that trigger a certain response. However noble strength and bravery may be, it is ignoble to seek excuses to flaunt them. When we do so, we reveal that strength and bravery are not our true nature, but merely public postures.

The people in Chuang Tzu's poem have no self-sustaining identity. They are wholly defined by the settings and relationships of the world of action. They equate selfhood with particular activities, and their vitality depends on being in places where they can play those roles. Put them in places where their competencies are not required, and they find themselves on the thin edge of nonbeing.

Though this kind of role-playing is widespread among us, I think Chuang Tzu is especially concerned with a class of people that we would call professionals—experts, philosophers, critics, politicians, lawyers, liturgists, business executives, and the like. If it was important in his time to diagnose the pathologies of professionalism, it is even more important in ours. Not only do we have more professionals who may do themselves damage, but any pathologies they may have are multiplied many times over in a society that has become so dependent on their skills.

As professionals, we like to define ourselves in ways that stress competence, high standards, an ethic of service, personal sacrifice, and so on. But in "Active Life" Chuang Tzu is examining the shadow side of professional activity, and he would probably propose a different definition: A professional is a person who has invested long hours and much money to develop an allegedly rare ability that others can be convinced to need and to purchase at a high price. Admittedly partial, such a definition points to the ways that we professionals get caught in the "world of objects" that Chuang Tzu describes, in the spinning of those interlocked illusions that too often trap the professional and the society in a vicious circle of nonsense.

Becoming a professional requires an investment of time and money that can easily set the vicious circle in motion. We have a myth in our society that the more education one has, the more choices one can make. True, more education may lead to more affluence and hence to more consumer choices, but more education may also narrow the range of meaningful choices about the directions of our lives. Once you have spent ten years and a small fortune getting a medical degree, how can you choose to be a logger if you discover that logging is what you really want to do? If we had perfect self-discernment before we began professional training, and we got trained in our hearts' desires, all would be well. But we lack such prescience. It often takes years for our hearts to speak, and when they do we often cannot hear them, having been deafened by the system that Chuang Tzu describes.

Our deafness may have begun well before we were trained. Some of us pursued professional training largely because of expectations that had surrounded our lives since childhood. Parents, friends, and the pressures of subcultures may have conditioned our decisions before we reached an age of self-determination; only years later do we realize that we are living out other people's dreams for our lives, not our own. Becoming a "prisoner in the world of objects" can begin at an early age behind the benign guise of parental encouragement to "aim high." In that very encouragement parents sometimes make objects of their children, treating them as extensions of the parents' own lives, as agents of fulfillment for the parents' unrealized dreams. When we start life that way, as objects to be shaped in ways that please our makers, we may well get trapped in the object-world and become object-makers ourselves.

In fact, the full-fledged professional has the power and sometimes the necessity to extend the world of objects even further, to make objects of other people. As John McKnight has so persuasively argued, the professions too often promote themselves by creating clients who have problems that only the professionals can solve.[5] As Chuang Tzu might have put it, What would become of professionals if their clients disappeared?

If the idea of professionals "creating" people with problems seems ludicrous, here is a recent example from my own hometown. A private firm decided to build a fifty-bed psychiatric facility and staff it with therapists, psychiatric nurses, and related mental health workers. Some people were excited; the project would bring new development, tax dollars, employment for construction workers as well as for permanent staff. But others had reservations. There was no demonstrated need for a new facility of this sort, no survey indicating that the community either had, or was likely to discover, fifty or more people who needed psychiatric care but would not otherwise receive it. These critics argued that as soon as the facility was built and staffed there would be great pressure in the mental health system to "create" fifty mentally ill people to occupy its rooms.

Of course, the critics did not mean that the system would demonically invade the lives of fifty "normal" citizens and drive them crazy (though some would say that every system has its ways of doing exactly that). Their point was simply that with fifty well-advertised beds standing empty, psychiatrists would be more likely to recommend hospitalization to people that they would have sent home under other circumstances—perhaps even lowering their threshold definition of who is mentally ill, a slippery concept at best. In this sense, professionals can "create" clients, not by the exercise of godlike powers, but by the exercise of simple self-interest and the logic of professional necessity.

That necessity is partly economic—the fifty beds must be filled to recoup the cost of building the clinic—but it is deeply personal as well. What meaning would life have for some mental health professionals if there were not people who depended on their help? The threat to personal meaning is easily as powerful as a threat to income in driving us professionals to "create" the clients we need.

This personal dynamic can be amplified many times over by the guild structures that every profession develops to protect and promote its interests. How many psychiatrists will publicly challenge their peers on the ways that they "create" clients, when to do so would result in fewer referrals at best and isolation from the guild at worst? I know of no profession that does not have the shadow side that Chuang Tzu describes: a silent conspiracy to stay in business by making sure that society never runs out of the problems that guild members know how to solve.

One tactic in that conspiracy is to name and analyze our problems in a language so mystifying that only trained professionals can understand it. Such language is characteristic of every profession from ministry to metallurgy, and the mental health profession is no exception. When society at large is schooled to think of elemental human sadness as a "depressive syndrome," what layperson has the confidence to offer its victims help? Instead, we turn to the very professionals whose opaque language helps to keep them in power by making laypeople feel inadequate.

Of course, the "client population" is often in on the conspiracy to keep professionals in business. There would be less pathology among mental health professionals if we did not turn to them for so many needs, if we did not yield to them so many of our powers of self-healing. There was a time when some mental health crises (grieving, for example) were cared for by the lay community rather than by trained therapists. But as we have abandoned the responsibilities of community, we have lost its benefits as well, and the only friend some people can find is one they pay by the hour.

The irony of the pathology of professionalism is that the word *professional* originally had a very different meaning. At root, a professional is *one who makes a profession of faith*—faith in something larger and wiser than his or her own powers. The true professional is the opposite of someone who makes objects of other people by creating dependencies. Instead, the true professional is a person whose action points beyond his or her self to that underlying reality, that hidden wholeness, on which we all can rely. The grieving person does not need professional technique so much as a restored confidence in the elemental grace of life, the grace found in community or in nature or in the self. The true professional is one who does not obscure that grace with illusions of technical prowess, but one who strips away all illusions to reveal a reliable truth in which the human heart can rest.

III. ACTION AS SELF-FULFILLING PROPHECY

The reactive life as portrayed by Chuang Tzu is not only untrue to the nature of things. Even worse, it has the power to create self-fulfilling prophecies, layer upon layer of social and psychological illusions that become more real to us than the reality they obscure. Many of our most fervent convictions about the nature of the world we live in (e.g., the notion that it's a tough world out there, and you have to be tough to survive it) are not accurate reflections of the world as it is given, so much as "realities" created by our convictions themselves.

The classic example of a self-fulfilling prophecy involves the collapse of a perfectly healthy bank. If people start spreading the false rumor that this bank will soon run out of cash and be unable to pay its creditors, account holders will line up around the block to withdraw their money before it is too late. The result, of course, if that the false rumor soon becomes true; as more and more misled people withdraw their cash the bank becomes unable to meet its debts. Action based on false beliefs has the power to bring those falsehoods into being.

We do well to examine the assumptions behind our actions to see if we are giving birth to "realities" we would rather not have. Look again, for example, at some of the actors in Chuang Tzu's poem. The expert who is unhappy without problems to vex him spends a lifetime fostering vexations. The philosopher who pines away if her teaching is never attacked goes around creating attackers. The brave woman who needs an emergency to show bravery precipitates more emergencies in the world. The swordsman who wants a battle will escalate as many encounters as he can into excuses to swing his sword.

It is no trick to find negative examples of such self-fulfilling prophecies in the world outside Chuang Tzu's poem. An exact parallel to the swordsman, for example, is found in our military-industrial complex, in the dependence of our economy on war or preparedness for war, in the fact that our complex and expensive doomsday weapons cry out daily to be used. Our society is filled with people and institutions who require a battle to fulfill their sense of meaning. Sooner or later their requirements will become self-fulfilling prophecies.

Another example of prophecy that makes illusion into reality is in the daily assault called advertising. A product that no one really needs becomes a "must" for large numbers of people simply because advertising has the power to make them believe they need it. Ads create a social climate in which people feel deprived if they do not have X, so more and more X is sold, thus creating more and more consumers who must have it. As Chuang Tzu says, "What would become of business without a market of fools?"

If action can bring illusion into reality, so can inaction. Take, for example, our common tendency, especially in the midst of complex institutions, to believe "There is nothing I can do about this problem because of the politics of the situation." We imagine that "the politics" is some mysterious force outside us, when, in fact, it is no more than the network of decisions made daily by us and by others, decisions regarding what we care about and whether we will act on those concerns. When we fail to act because of the complexities of "politics," we yield our power to others, and another self-fulfilling prophecy has been fulfilled. Then "the politics of the situation" *does* become a mysterious force outside us, in which we have no voice, and the problem that bothers us is likely to get worse.

It is easy to name real-world parallels to the negative prophecies that fulfill themselves in Chuang Tzu's poem. But it is more difficult to name parallels to the positive examples that Chuang Tzu offers, possibly because they strike closer to home. Some of us have no doubt that ad agencies or the military-industrial complex are up to their eyebrows in the business of making illusions into dubious realities. But what about "the benevolent, the dutiful," who "are always looking for chances to display virtue?" Is it possible that some of the apparent goodness in the world (perhaps even some that you and I try to create) is as much a product of self-fulfilling prophecies as is some of the evil? And if so, is there anything wrong with that, as long as goodness is the result?

Yes, some of the world's apparent goodness results from our need to "display virtue"; and yes, there is something wrong with that, or so it seems to me. Some of us harbor an inner *do-gooder* who needs to act benevolently not so much for the sake of others as for the sake of self-promotion. We are like one of the first religious groups to arrive in this country, of whom it has been said, "They came to do good and ended up doing well."

The question is always, Good for whom? I do not mean that acts that are good for the actor cannot be good for other people; in fact, I doubt that an act can be good for others if the actor is not nurtured by it. But "goodness" that is driven primarily by the actor's needs is unlikely to be good at all. Such goodness is often imposed on people who have no desire for it, people who become the objects of the actor's self-serving charity. For those recipients the experience is not one of benevolence but of violence, the violence that is done whenever someone else decides what you need without consulting you.

Such action is ultimately wrong, whatever its intentions, because it is not organic, not in the true nature of things. Instead, it is a forced goodness and force always turns subjects into objects, making benefactor and beneficiary alike prisoners in the object-world. Ultimately good acts are those that allow people the freedom to choose their own destinies; at least, that is how I understand the ultimate goodness of the God who created us to be free. This freedom includes the other person's freedom to choose hell in a handbasket, whether or not I approve. It does not include imposition of my moral will in a way that imprisons my sister or brother.

There is an ancient parable about these matters, whose outcome has always seemed dubious to me. A wise man was walking the banks of a flood-swollen river when he saw a scorpion tangled in the roots near the water's edge. Knowing that the scorpion would soon drown in the rising waters, he reached down to rescue it, only to be stung viciously every time his hand came near the creature. A passerby berated the wise man for his foolishness, but the wise man replied, "Just because it is in the scorpion's nature to sting, why should I abandon my nature to save?"

The problem with the wise man's response is in his assumption that the scorpion's sting was a reflex reaction rather than an intentional act meaning, "I don't want to be rescued!" I can identify with the scorpion, as can anyone who has ever been "rescued" against his or her will. It would be a better story if the deepest nature of the wise man was not to rescue automatically, no matter what the situation, but to listen to the truth of the other and respond accordingly.

Not only would such responsiveness make a better story, but it would make us better people, make for a better world. The world does not need more saviors who impose their versions of salvation on others, nor does it need more scorpions who are bitter about being saved and are prepared to sting again. Self-fulfilling prophecies, whether they appear to be for good or for ill, always bring us ill in the long run, simply because they are always substitutes for that underlying reality that is our only ground and hope.

IV. ON MAKING A LIFE FOR OURSELVES

Perhaps the most powerful moment in Chuang Tzu's "Active Life" comes toward the end of the poem, when he says, "Produce! Get results! Make money! Make friends! Make changes! Or you will die of despair!" In those few words he sums up our breathless, frantic version of the active life, a life in which we continually run scared that we are not *making* enough of this or that, enough of whatever it is that will justify, or even save, us. Much of what Chuang Tzu finds pitiful about this version of the active life is summed up in the notion that we must "make" our lives.

Alan Watts offers a pointed example of how deeply the idea of making is driven into our Western worldview. He says,

It's quite natural for a child brought up in Western culture to say to its mother, "How was I made?" We think that's a very logical thing to ask . . . But actually this is a question that I don't think would be asked by a Chinese child. It wouldn't occur. The Chinese child might say, "How did I grow?" But certainly not, "How was I made?"[6]

Think of how often the idea of making occurs in everyday discourse. We speak, as Chuang Tzu says, of making money, making friends, making changes. We also speak of making time, making love, making peace, making a deal, making our way, making a mark, making things right, making meaning, making a living, and—to cover all the bases—making "it." Even Yeats, that virtuoso of the English language, wrote of our "soul-making." When a verb is so pervasive in ordinary conversation and when we join it to so many nouns that represent such diverse phenomena, that verb must reveal something essential in our view of ourselves, our action, and our world. What are we to "make" of it?

Clearly, we regard ourselves as the manufacturers of nearly everything under the sun, including things that we cannot possibly make. I suppose we can make a deal or make a mark. But can we really make things right, or make peace, or make love? And surely no one, no matter how smart or skillful, can make time. We seem to regard much of the world as raw material that waits passively to be given shape by our own designs and energies; in fact, the word *make* comes from a root that relates to the kneading of clay or dough. Karl Marx, whose basic orientation to the world is found as much among capitalists as among communists, spoke of human labor as "adding value" to raw materials, as if the material world had no value in itself. Unless you write all of this off as "mere language" (and I do not believe language is ever mere), you have to conclude that we unconsciously imagine ourselves as the ultimate makers of nearly everything, including our own lives.

For some years I have had a cartoon posted above my desk to remind me of how ludicrous this version of activism is. It shows a vast, flat plain stretching off into the distant horizon, with only a few rocks and scrubby plants scattered across it. There are numerous small groups of people out on the plain, working the ground with pickaxes, shovels, and wheelbarrows, while in the foreground stand two people with blueprints who are supervising the work. The caption under the cartoon reads, "Early Work on the Grand Canyon."[7] (Having looked at and laughed at that cartoon for years, I was reminded, during a recent rafting trip through the Grand Canyon, that some people want to dam the Colorado River and fill the canyon to generate hydroelectric power. Only so, they believe, could this magnificent gorge be of real value. Sometimes the distance between a cartoon and the real world is shockingly short.)

We will better understand the source of this strange bias if we explore its opposite—the conviction that we do not make the world or ourselves, but instead receive life as it is given. This is the conviction behind that great passage in the Book of Job in which God is trying to impress Job with the foolishness of regarding his life as anything other than a gift: "Where were you when I laid the earth's foundations? . . . Who decided the dimensions of it, do you know?" (Job 38:4–5, JB). Despite our pretensions, there are some things we simply cannot make. Why do some of us have such a hard time accepting that elemental and obvious fact?

If we were to accept large areas of life as pure gift, we would be forced to acknowledge that we are not in control. Were we to live as recipients rather than makers, we might feel dependent and diminished, like clients of some cosmic welfare system that demeans our lives. If we were to affirm that we have received many gifts, that we have not earned all that we have, we might feel obliged to pass the gifts along rather than hoard our treasures to ourselves. To acknowledge that we do not and cannot make most of what we have would strip us of too many illusions and take us too close to reality for comfort.

It seems odd, but the despair that Chuang Tzu speaks of descends on some of us in this society of "makers" when we are forced to admit our dependence on gifts. In that moment we are compelled to face our own limits and reliances, compelled to admit that total self-sufficiency is, and always has been, an illusion. In that moment some of us do not feel the liberation of burdens being lifted; we feel disillusionment and despair.

But Chuang Tzu knows that this despair is a step on the journey toward joy. He knows that real despair comes from clinging to the conviction that if I cannot "make meaning" for my life—by making money, friends, changes—there is no meaning to life at all. True despair is the refusal to recognize the fragility of all our efforts at making, the ease with which our making is destroyed by error, evil, illness, age, death. The joy beyond despair comes when we abandon the exhausting illusion of self-sufficiency and become the grateful recipients of the gifts that life provides.

I have known so many people, especially men, who fall into despair when their "active lives" end at retirement. They withdraw from the work they have been doing, and it is as if they had withdrawn their hands from a pool of water: The water closes up as if their hands had never been there. True despair is the failure to learn before we die that the water eventually closes up over everything, that we never manage to leave the indelible marks of our dreams. But once we learn that, and once the gifts of life are acknowledged, we can proceed to be makers in new and more hopeful ways.

For the fact is that we will always need to be makers. There *is* raw material in our lives, and it can be properly worked and shaped; in fact, the chance to work it is one of our major gifts. The fact that we lead gifted lives does not mean that everything we need comes down like manna from heaven. There is a legitimate sense in which we need to make roads and houses and dinner, even friends and a living and love. But we need to look again at the truth of how we make, to see how intricately our making is interlaced with our gifts. We have the gift of the raw material itself, which we did not manufacture. We have the gift of freedom to imagine shapes that this material might take. We have the gift of skills and tools to do the making, and the gift of the power to use them. If we can understand our giftedness, our making will no longer carry the burden of impossibility that leads finally to despair.

At this moment, I am engaged in active making, the making of this book. I know that I bring a certain effort to this work, including twenty-five years of trying to learn how to write. But in my more perceptive moments, I am aware of the many unearned gifts that interact with my making of a text— gifts of insight, of illustration, of language, of sheer grace. Though I experience joy in the hard work of writing, my joy would be diminished were it not for these unbidden gifts.

Even so, I and others I know have difficulty integrating the idea of giftedness into our self-image as makers. Western culture has a million ways of reinforcing the illusion that the world consists of inert stuff *out there* and that we are the active agents of change whose role is to get that stuff into shape. This is the assumption that has fueled the rapid development of technology. This is the assumption on which most modern education has been based, an education aimed at giving us the tools to exercise dominion over the earth.

But now philosophers of science have begun to discard the arrogant notion of an inert world *out there* that is discovered and manipulated by an active intelligence that resides *in here,* in us. According to the new view, all of reality is active and interactive, a vast web of mutual relationships. We can no longer maintain the old distinction between an active knower and an inactive world. As knowers we both act and are acted upon, and reality as we know it is the outcome of an infinitely complex encounter between ourselves and our environment.

In this encounter we do some shaping, to be sure, but we are also shaped by the relational reality of which we are a part. We are part, and only a part, of the great community of creation. If we can act in ways that embrace this fact, ways that honor the gifts we receive through our membership in this community, we can move beyond the despair that comes when we believe that our act is the only act in town. Even more important, our action will less likely lead to corporate despair and more likely contribute to the health of the web of being and of all who live in that web. When authentic action replaces unconscious reaction, the active life becomes not (in the words of Chuang Tzu) "a pity," but a vital and creative power.

4. "The Woodcarver": A Model for Right Action

I. THE TAO OF ACTION

If the poem "Active Life" were our only evidence, we might conclude that Chuang Tzu and Taoism simply scorn the life of action. Some Westerners misinterpret Taoism in this way, imagining that it counsels a go-with-the-flow passivity that disdains responsibility and real work. This impression is compounded by the fact that Chuang Tzu and other Taoist teachers frequently speak approvingly of *wu-wei,* a word often translated as *inaction.* But *wu-wei* does not mean inaction, and Taoism does not preach passivity. Instead, both point to what we might call *right action,* a form of action that is at once more disciplined and more liberating than the frenzy that we in the West often equate with active life.

The Way of Chuang Tzu contains a number of prose poems and stories that convey the Taoist sense of right action simply by portraying people in the midst of working, creating, caring. My favorite is the tale of Khing, the master woodcarver.

"The Woodcarver"

Khing, the master carver, made a bell stand
Of precious wood. When it was finished,
All who saw it were astounded. They said it must be
The work of spirits.
The Prince of Lu said to the master carver:
"What is your secret?"

Khing replied: "I am only a workman:
I have no secret. There is only this:

When I began to think about the work you commanded
I guarded my spirit, did not expend it
On trifles, that were not to the point.
I fasted in order to set
My heart at rest.
After three days fasting, I had forgotten gain and success.
After five days
I had forgotten praise or criticism.
After seven days
I had forgotten my body
With all its limbs.

"By this time all thought of your Highness
And of the court had faded away.
All that might distract me from the work
Had vanished.
I was collected in the single thought
Of the bell stand.

"Then I went to the forest
To see the trees in their own natural state.
When the right tree appeared before my eyes,
The bell stand also appeared in it, clearly, beyond doubt.
All I had to do was to put forth my hand
And begin.

"If I had not met this particular tree
There would have been
No bell stand at all.

"What happened?
My own collected thought
Encountered the hidden potential in the wood;
From this live encounter came the work
Which you ascribe to the spirits."[1]

If we are tempted to write off "Active Life" as too cynical about the world of action, we may be equally tempted to dismiss "The Woodcarver" as too romantic. On the surface, this story seems to portray a person very unlike most of us, an expert who has the luxury of acting in a context more benign than most of our workplaces. The woodcarver is an artisan engaged in the creation of beauty. He seems to be surrounded by people with deep aesthetic sense. And, wonder of wonders, he seems to have permission to take time off in the midst of his work to slow down and meditate. We, however, may not feel masterful at what we do; the people around us may not appreciate our work; and we certainly cannot take a week off to gain vision and to focus our energies!

But dismissing this story as too romantic is simply a way of distancing ourselves from its teaching, a way of shielding our own active lives from the story's scrutiny. As we move inside the story we will find that the woodcarver is not unlike us, his context not unlike our own. In fact, the pressures surrounding the woodcarver turn out to be more severe than those in my work setting—and, I suspect, in yours as well.

Many people feel hampered by the hierarchies in which we often must work, by institutional structures that curtail the independence that we think we need to do our creative best. But few people work in a setting as demanding as the woodcarver's. He lives in a feudal society of princes and peasants, and his "boss," the Prince of Lu, is very near the top of that rigid and unyielding order. When I ask Chinese scholars what would have happened if Khing had failed to produce a bell stand acceptable to the prince, they usually answer with a sweeping movement of the forefinger across the front of the throat. Khing was under considerable pressure to do the job and to do it right, on penalty of his life. It is unlikely that the prince had a personnel handbook with an employee grievance procedure in case things failed to work out. So the freedom of action Khing has in the story cannot be attributed to an enlightened employer.

But what about the fact that Khing is a "master carver," a craftsman who presumably has higher skills than most of us? Does this not make him special, exempt from the conditions that confine us amateurs? Once again our defensiveness is showing. We want to believe that we are so ordinary compared to "the experts," that our action cannot possibly be as free and graceful as theirs, that we cannot be held to those standards. But, as I shall explore later, one of the critical moments in the story comes when Khing says, "I am only a workman: I have no secret." The quality of his action comes not primarily through his expertise but through his willingness to claim his common humanity, a claim that all of us, however amateur, can make.

Having meditated on "The Woodcarver" for years, I have come to see four critical junctures in the story. At each of these points a vital element of action is revealed, and the way we relate to each element determines the quality of our action. The four elements are motives, skills and gifts, "the other," and results. The woodcarver transforms his relation to each of these elements in a way that frees him from reaction in the world of objects, frees him to engage in *wu-wei,* rightly understood—in action that is harmonious with his own reality and with the reality around him. The woodcarver offers us a model of right action.

II. MOTIVES

If we want to break out of the mechanistic and obsessive sort of action criticized in "Active Life," we must first learn to ask ourselves a simple question: "Why am I doing this?" This is the question of motives, and we hardly ever ask it of ourselves (though we are sometimes quick to inspect, and suspect, the motives of other people). Every action has some motive behind it, some impetus, a force-field out of which it arises. If we do not explore that force we will never act in a transcendent way; we will live out our active lives as automatons who move but do not choose.

Why did the woodcarver set out to create a bell stand? Again, it is easy to read the story romantically and imagine that Khing is a dreamy artist creating "art for art's sake." But that would grossly distort a story that tells us that Khing set out to make the bell stand because the Prince of Lu commanded him to do it. The threat of the Prince's command and his potential displeasure hangs over the woodcarver's work like the sword of Damocles. As the woodcarver's action proceeds from this initial point of coercion, it does move toward the freedom of art for art's sake. But this is not a freedom granted by the prince or some other external authority. It is a freedom the woodcarver claims for himself, on his own inner authority.

Many of us act from motives that are not entirely benign, on terms that are not always our own. We may act, not by choice, but on demand; not for ourselves and our own reasons, but for others and their reasons; not for the sake of the act itself, but for the sake of the money or security or approval or prestige it will bring; not because we love working, but because we want to avoid the guilt of not working. Motives such as these are so common that we accept them as the inevitable launching pads of action.

But a launching pad is only temporary; once launched, the rocket is free of the pad's constraints. We often must launch our actions from motives and circumstances that are less than ideal. If we wait for the ideal motives before we act, most of us would never act; but if we allow our action to be confined by its original motives, our action may be slipshod, graceless, banal. What is the process by which we, like the woodcarver, might accept an undesirable impetus to action and yet allow our action to be transformed into something of beauty and truth that transcends its original constraints?

I suspect that the woodcarver began by understanding that sometimes we must be outwardly called to our own inward truth, and that these callings may come from the most unlikely sources—such as a ruthless prince. The call may come from the wrong place or for the wrong reason, but that does not mean that it is the wrong call.

A friend of mine tells the story of arriving at college for the opening of his freshman year, working all day to get moved in, going to bed that night and waking up the next morning with the thought, The only reason I'm in college is because my parents wanted it, and that's not good enough. So he started packing up and moving out, but the job took the whole day and he had to sleep in the dorm again that night. When he woke up the next morning he thought, So what? My parents' desire for me to be here is as good a reason as any—and so he decided to stay. Obviously, he had gotten in touch with his own inner call to be in college, however inarticulate, and had transcended the external factors that had "forced" him to be there.

My friend was probably so afraid of the challenges of college that he railed against his parents as a way of evading his own fears. Such fears rise up in almost every form of action. We know that the woodcarver began his work fearfully, for he says, "I fasted in order to set my heart at rest," clearly indicating that his heart was agitated at first by the threat of the prince's command. The story of the woodcarver is instructive, not because he is fearless (which would make him very unlike most of us), but because he did not let his fears paralyze him. Instead, he walked into and through those fears that he could not get out of, and found the freedom to act on the other side.

The process by which the woodcarver found his freedom is more deliberate and disciplined than the process my friend went through, but at bottom it is the same: a process of contemplation by which we penetrate the illusion of enslavement and claim our own inner liberty. In the woodcarver's case, that process is called fasting. Taken literally, of course, fasting means abstaining from food. It is a discipline that requires us to override deep biological impulses of survival, to override the social conditioning that links eating with well-being. Through fasting, the body and, some say, the soul are purged of poisons and brought back to health.

We could read this story as an exhortation to clarify our action by abstaining from food for a while, and people who have tried that know that it can help. But Chuang Tzu has a larger lesson to teach. He opens up the metaphorical meaning of fasting by paralleling it with *forgetting*. The key to the woodcarver's contemplation is that it enabled him to forget and therefore abstain from all sorts of psychic "junk food"— gain and success, praise and criticism, and even the Prince of Lu and his court.

The woodcarver's real fasting is his active refusal to ingest, to internalize, the poisoned baits that can kill the spirit of right action. Not only did the woodcarver fend off the allures of material gain, higher status, immunity from criticism, and guaranteed praise, but he even resisted the temptation to toady to his all-powerful employer, the prince. By the time he had fasted for seven days, he says, " . . . all thought of your Highness / And of the court had faded away. / All that might distract me from the work / Had vanished."

It is a splendid moment in the story. Imagine that your boss asks you, "How did you manage to do this job so well?" and you respond, "Well, frankly, I simply forgot that you even exist!" At every possible level the woodcarver worked to forget the externals so that he could remember his inner truth.

I am struck by the centrality of forgetting in this story because I tend to do just the opposite when I am poised to act. I strain to recall everything—what I am doing, why I am doing it, who I am doing it for, how to do it, when it needs to be done, what the outcomes should be. For example, in my early years of teaching I spent hours and hours before each class re-reading key books, writing and rewriting lecture notes, reviewing, rehearsing, remembering. But this sort of preparation did not make me a good teacher. Too often it stuffed me so full of external ideas and strategies, so full of myself, that I was unable to hear my students' questions and interests and needs, let alone respond to them. I had ingested so many externals that my teaching was leaden and graceless. Like the archer in the following Chuang Tzu poem, I wanted so desperately to do a good job that in my desperation I botched it.

"The Need to Win"

When an archer is shooting for nothing
He has all his skill.

If he shoots for a brass buckle
He is already nervous.
If he shoots for a prize of gold
He goes blind
Or sees two targets—
He is out of his mind!

His skill has not changed. But the prize
Divides him. He cares.
He thinks more of winning
Than of shooting—
And the need to win
Drains him of power.[2]

Of course, there is a phase in the development of any art or craft when we are still trying to learn it, and so we must remember what we are doing. Khing was not always a master woodcarver; there was a time when he had to ponder long over which chisel to use, a time when he needed to recall how he had mangled his last project so that he could avoid making the same mistake again. But once we have learned we must paradoxically forget, trusting that our hard-won knowledge will arise when needed without our forcing it.

The forgetting of the woodcarver is like that of the major league shortstop who has no time to remember as he sweeps to his left to scoop up a hard grounder; or like that of a concert pianist who cannot afford to be encumbered by remembering as her fingers negotiate the rapids of a Bach fugue; or like that of the master surgeon who told her students that at one point in open-heart surgery, "You have only thirty seconds to tie off this artery—so you have got to take your time." Right action requires knowledge, but if we try to remember all that we know, that very knowledge can paralyze our action.

By forgetting what he knew about his craft and his context, the woodcarver paradoxically was able to remember the one thing most important to right action: his own inner truth, his own nature. The word *remember* literally means to *re*-member, to reunite that hidden wholeness in us and in our world that is so easily torn apart by powers within and around us. The woodcarver refuses to allow himself and his action to be *dis-membered* by the forces of fragmentation. Through fasting and forgetting, he says, "All that might distract me from the work / Had vanished. / I was collected in the single thought / Of the bell stand." He does not say that he worked to "collect his thoughts" in the way that I might, but that he allowed himself to be "collected." Through fasting and forgetting he allowed himself and his world to be regathered into their original unity, to be re-membered, re-called, re-collected into that hidden wholeness that is the only context for right action.

There is another word that may describe the woodcarver's path to transcendence even better than *fasting* and *forgetting.* It is *dying.* By the final day of his fast, Khing says, "I had forgotten my body with all its limbs." I do not think he is telling us to ignore our bodies or try to discard them; people who fast often care more for their bodies than those of us who never abstain. Instead, I think Khing is moving beyond his sense of bodily separateness and allowing himself to be absorbed into the whole. This is death and why we fear it—the loss of our boundaries and distinctiveness, the annihilation of self. Driven by this fear, we act over and against things to prove our separateness, and in the process our action becomes adversarial, fragmenting us and our world, destroying the hidden wholeness.

The fear of dying must have been in the woodcarver, especially since the command that gave rise to his work carried an implicit death threat from the omnipotent prince. But the woodcarver, knowing that no one can get out of death, deals with his fear by walking directly into it. He fasts and forgets, denying himself the external resources that we commonly regard as necessary for survival. In the process he discovers the inner resources necessary for authentic life; he is re-membered to the hidden wholeness; he creates a work of surpassing beauty. And it all began with the prince's high-handed and threatening command. If we are to transcend the motives and contexts that so often limit and distort our action, we must enter into our own versions of fasting, forgetting, and dying.

III. SKILLS AND GIFTS

The skill necessary to act is the second element of action that the woodcarver transcends and transforms in the course of his story. Khing is described as a "master carver," a status he could attain only through years of hard work. Having invested so much time and energy in learning his craft, he might have been tempted to use his *mastery* in the negative sense of that word: a process of forcing something or someone into slavery to serve one's own ends. Khing must have been tempted to assume that he knew it all, that his long years of experience had conferred on him the right to envision the perfect bell stand and force that vision onto the tree. After all, he had worked hard to attain the status and power of an expert. Why not go ahead and do whatever he wanted to do?

The story suggests that Khing was surrounded by the sort of adulation that can easily tempt experts toward an inflated sense of self. "All who saw [the bell stand] were astounded. They said it must be / The work of spirits." And the Prince of Lu, Khing's employer, further tempts the woodcarver toward a sense of superiority when he asks, "What is your secret?"

But the woodcarver will have none of it. With a candor that can come only from deep self-knowledge, he deflects all this praise and puffery by saying, "I am only a workman: I have no secret." He insists on the humanness of his work and refuses to shroud it in mystique.

What a contrast there is between this candid woodcarver and some of the "masters" of our time who thrive on mystifying the public about what they do and how they do it. By guarding their secrets and pretending to have secrets where they don't, some professionals try to protect their markets from laypeople who might do for themselves what the experts do for a price. But Khing has no need to aggrandize his own mastery in ways that discourage other people from discovering theirs.

The question is, Why do so many people want to be mystified by expertise? Why are the people around Khing convinced that his bell stand "must be the work of spirits" rather than of human agency? Why does the Prince of Lu ask Khing for his "secret" rather than affirming Khing for his gifts and his hard work?

Perhaps jealousy is at work here. Perhaps neither the people nor the prince want to give Khing his due because their own work seems so inferior to his. But perhaps the deeper reason for their response is not jealousy but fear. By spiritualizing and mystifying Khing's action, the people and the prince distance themselves from it and evade the challenge implicit in its very humanness. If they were to embrace the notion that Khing is "only a workman" who has no secrets (which Khing clearly wants them to do), they would have to reflect upon and revitalize their own active lives. Instead, they let themselves off the hook by attributing the bell stand to something other than Khing's hard work and his faithfulness to his gifts.

Sadly, some contemporary spirituality errs this way with its notion that anything good that we do is clearly the work of "the Spirit." Behind such language often lurks the idea that it is egotistical to claim our work as our own. But an authentic spirituality of action will celebrate our desire and capacity to co-create the world with the gifts we have been given.

In my experience, more people suffer from a sense of incompetence or impotence than enjoy feelings of superiority about their powers of creation. In a world where so many people feel unable to do a masterwork, the story of the master carver can seem utterly irrelevant: "I have no special skills. I am the master of nothing. How can this fairy tale possibly have a bearing on my life? I could never achieve the beauty of the bell stand in anything I do."

There is good news for the person who feels this way, but the good news contains the very challenge that the prince and the people were trying to evade: Every human being is born with some sort of gift, an inclination or an instinct that can become a full-blown mastery. We may not see our gift for what it is. Having seen it we may choose not to accept the gift and its consequences for our lives. Or, having claimed our gift, we may not be willing to do the hard work necessary to nurture it. But none of these evasions can alter the fact that the gift is ours. Each of us is a master at something, and part of becoming fully alive is to discover and develop our birthright competence.

Discerning our native gifts is difficult for many reasons. We live in a culture that tells us there is no such thing as a gift, that we must earn or make everything we get. Social forces such as racism, sexism, and ageism press poor self-images upon us. Various inner pathologies may lead us to embrace those images despite the obvious damage they do. But the most subtle barrier to the discernment of our native gifts is in the gifts themselves: They are so central to us, so integral to who we are, that we take them for granted and are often utterly unaware of the mastery they give us.

The skills we are most aware of possessing are often those we have acquired only through long hours of study and practice, at considerable financial or personal cost. Precisely because these skills once cost us effort to acquire, and still cost us effort to employ, we are acutely aware of owning them. Ironically, these self-conscious skills are often not our leading strengths; if they were, they would not be so effortful. But they are the strengths upon which we sometimes build our identities and our careers—though we build on an anxious, uncertain foundation. Meanwhile, our native, instinctive gifts either languish unused and unappreciated or get used unconsciously without being named and claimed.

Our tendency to identify ourselves with our acquired skills rather than our natural gifts is one of the less desirable habits of the ego. It is the ego that decides what skills it prizes, the ego that exerts the effort to develop those skills, the ego that manipulates and markets those skills once it acquires them. Because the ego's identity is so heavily invested in these acquired skills, it does not want to acknowledge the natural, untrained, effortless gifts over which the ego has no ownership or control. Indeed, the very fact that we have gifts that the ego did nothing to earn is threatening to the ego, which desperately needs to believe that nothing comes into being without its own authorization or agency. In fact, the ego can sometimes be so insistent on its status that it would sooner diminish us than be humbled by our gifts. If we have no formal training, no acquired skills, the ego may insist that we have no competence at all rather than honor our native gifts.

We need ego-strength to live and live fruitfully. But it is a paradoxical truth that in order to gain the strength that comes from knowing our gifts we may have to fight the ego's drive to dominate our lives. The woodcarver fought through fasting, forgetting, and dying to the false demands of his ego. In that process he penetrated the ego's self-delusions and arrived at a truth about himself, his gifts, and his relation to the reality around him, a truth that allowed him to transcend the traps inherent in the skillfulness necessary for action.

It is important to realize that the woodcarver's native gift may not have been the obvious one—his capacity to employ woodworking tools with consummate skill. Even if he had been born with the manual dexterity that woodworking requires, his skill with those particular tools surely took him years of practice to perfect. A careful reading of the story shows that the woodcarver possesses several other gifts, all of which are essential to the mastery he demonstrates: the capacity to wait patiently for insight to emerge, the capacity to trust in the outcomes of an uncertain process, the capacity to take risks even under pressure, the capacity to speak his truth even when it is not what people want to hear. Any of these may be his birthright gift, without which his technical ability to carve would make him no more than an average artisan.

So when we seek our own birthright gifts, it is important not to equate them with the techniques our society names as skills. Our gifts may be as simple as a real interest in other people, a quiet and caring manner, an eye for beauty, a love of rhythm and sound. But in those simple personal gifts the seeds of vocation are often found, if we are willing to do the inner and outer work necessary to cultivate our mastery.

Some readers may remain unconvinced that everyone is born with some gift, some mastery. For them—wounded perhaps by an ego or a culture that says people are incompetent without training—the notion that we are all given expertise at birth may sound like the largest illusion of all. I cannot offer definitive proof of this claim for people who do not intuit its truth, but I can offer some supportive evidence.

Over the past decade a new approach to vocation seeking has emerged that draws on the insights of *depth psychology*.[3] In this approach people are encouraged to begin, not with their credentials, but with the question, "What are my leading gifts and abilities?" There are various ways to answer this question, but many of the new career counselors urge people to start by writing a childhood autobiography. Some job-seekers find it odd to be asked to explore their earliest childhood memories of how they spent time, what brought them pleasure, what they could not abide. How could this information possibly help one identify marketable adult skills?

What the exercise does, of course, is to circumvent the ego, to take us back to those days when we acted more from natural inclination than from the ego's images and demands. Some of the most powerful clues to our true gifts are buried deep in childhood, when we said and did and felt things without censoring them through external values or expectations. As we grow older, various social pressures may divert us from our native gifts, and we may experience much personal and vocational frustration as a result. But by recalling the activities that evoked our energies during childhood's innocence, we can get in touch with our own version of the woodcarver's mastery.

IV. THE OTHER

A third element of action that the woodcarver transcends and transforms is his relation to "the other." In the woodcarver's case the other is a tree, the wood that he carves. But every form of action involves an other. For a teacher it is students; for a doctor, patients; for a plumber, pipes; for a parent, the child; for a writer, words. In every action there is an other with which the actor is in partnership and on which the action in part depends.

The woodcarver's relation to the tree is obviously different from our society's relation to the physical world. For us, the world consists of raw material whose value depends almost entirely on our transforming it. But the woodcarver values the tree in and of itself. He knows that the tree has an identity and an integrity even as he himself does. He knows that if his work is to be true he must discern and keep faith with the nature of the tree. Where we would fell a thousand trees and make a thousand identical bell stands, the woodcarver enters into a "live encounter" with "this particular tree" that allows "the hidden potential in the wood" to emerge. So the action in this story does not belong to the woodcarver alone. It is a joint action, the result of a dynamic meeting between an actor and an other, and the bell stand that comes out of it is clearly a co-creation.

Chuang Tzu is not a romantic who tells us that the only right action is to leave everything alone, to leave nature untouched. For all his respect for the tree, the woodcarver still cuts it down and carves it up; the bell stand must be made. But in the midst of his realism Chuang Tzu insists that we must know and revere the nature of the other if our action is to be fruitful. This means giving up one of the most cherished but destructive myths of our technological society—the myth that all things are plastic, malleable, capable of being molded into any shape we require or desire. It is a myth at work in almost every sector of our lives.

Tired of your body? There is a diet or exercise program that promises to give you an entirely new shape. Tired of your personality? There is a therapy that promises to make you into a new person. Tired of the aimless meandering of that river? There is a technology that promises untold benefits from damming it up, creating a lake, generating hydroelectric power, and building resorts along the shore. Tired of the differences between cultures, of the threatening pretensions of cultures alien to your own? There is a military, economic, or political intervention that promises to make them just like us.

But these are false and destructive promises that can result only in violence to the other and to ourselves. Right action requires knowledge of the other's nature, which means knowledge of its potentials and limits, of what it can and cannot do. Good farmers know the nature of their soil; they know enough not to deplete it. Good teachers know the nature of their students; they know enough not to discourage them. Good mechanics know the nature of their machines; they know enough not to damage them. Good writers know the nature of words; they know enough not to stretch them out of shape. With such knowledge we can help the other fulfill its potentials, while respecting its limits, distorting neither the other nor ourselves as we act.

When we violate the nature of the other, we violate ourselves as well. At the very least, we despoil the environment that we ourselves inhabit. When we build dams in the wrong places, we diminish our own lives by destroying beauty and damaging the ecology. When we impose military "solutions" on alien societies, we make the world more dangerous for ourselves and for our descendants. When we force our values on our students or on our children, we create environments of hostility that corrode our own souls.

Sadly, destructive actions such as these tend to perpetuate themselves through vicious circles. Adults who have grown up with hostility tend to be hostile towards the young. People who have been victimized by the violence of their own culture tend to victimize those of other cultures. People who do not feel at home on earth tend to abuse the earth itself. So the key to action that knows and cares for the other is to know and care for ourselves.

That, of course, is exactly how the woodcarver came into fruitful relation with the tree—by knowing himself. He did not prepare for his work by conducting a scientific study of the external properties of trees, though his years of woodcarving clearly had given him knowledge of wood. He prepared by going into himself, by penetrating the illusions that had him in their grip (illusions about success and failure, for example) in order to touch his own truth. What he found inwardly was not an ego that wanted to impose its own designs on the tree, but a self that sought its rightful place in the scheme of things, its rightful relation to the prince, the people, the tree, and the task at hand. This is what the "live encounter" of right action is all about—an encounter between the inward truth of the actor and the inward truth of the other that penetrates all external appearances and expectations. If the actor lacks self-knowledge, the live encounter will never take place, and the action will be trapped in externals.

For example, one reason that we sometimes have bad teaching in our schools, teaching that does not touch and transform students, is that teachers are sometimes paralyzed by unexamined fears. They fear the ridicule of young people, the exposure of their own ignorance, the generational conflict of values, the loss of control. The authoritarian methods that bad teachers use—methods that put vast and arid distances between students and teachers and subjects—are unconscious attempts to keep these fears at bay. If such teachers understood themselves and their fears better, the result might be teaching that comes from within the teachers' self-knowledge and that makes learning into a live encounter once more.

Some people find the woodcarver's story flawed in the fact that the tree did not resist being cut and carved, while most of us work with people and systems that resist constantly. These critics wonder if the tree would have agreed to being cut down and carved into a bell stand if it had not been mute. They wonder how the woodcarver would have responded if the tree had been an animate object able to fight back.

No doubt this story would have had more punch for some of us if the other had been an unwieldy organization or a foot-dragging child. But anyone who has ever worked with wood knows that it is not mute, that it has a voice, a will, a nature. The story is not explicit about this, but in his carving Khing must have been listening and responding to the wood's voice, engaged in a dialogue of common language, despite the absence of vocal sounds. Had Khing not allowed the tree to tell him whether it wanted to become a bell stand and what kind of bell stand it wanted to become, no work of such surpassing beauty could have emerged.

The question is, How did Khing—and how do we—negotiate those moments of miscommunication, resistance, contradiction, and conflict that any live encounter is likely to involve? An answer is given in Chuang Tzu's "Cutting Up an Ox," the story of a butcher who is as skillful at his craft as Khing is at his. This butcher has used the same cleaver for nineteen years: "It has cut up a thousand oxen. Its edge is as keen now as if newly sharpened." The butcher's master, Prince Wan Hui, asks him how he could have cut up so many carcasses without dulling his blade, and the butcher responds,

> "There are spaces in the joints;
> The blade is thin and keen:
> When this thinness
> Finds that space
> There is all the room you need!
> It goes like a breeze!
> Hence I have this cleaver nineteen years
> As if newly sharpened!"

> "True, there are sometimes
> Tough joints. I feel them coming.
> I slow down, I watch closely
> Hold back, barely move the blade,

And whump! the part falls away
Landing like a clod of earth."

"Then I withdraw the blade,
I stand still
And let the joy of the work
Sink in.
I clean the blade
And put it away."

Prince Wan Hui said,
"This is it! My cook has shown me
How I ought to live
My own life!"[4]

When we are faced with a resistant other, we can respond the way the butcher does when he encounters a tough joint: He slows down, he watches closely, he holds back, he barely moves. He engages in a form of contemplative action that tries to discern the true nature of the other, action that does not attempt to accomplish its goals by main force. Despite the fact that the butcher is cutting up an ox, his action is essentially nonviolent, not unlike the contemplative actions with which Gandhi dissected the British Empire in India.

We can also find clues for our own action in the butcher's attitude before and after he acts. The butcher begins with a clear vision that "there are spaces in the joints," that he is not dealing with an impenetrable monolith that needs to be overwhelmed by brute force. There are such "spaces" in every person, every system, every problem, and seeing them is essential to right action of every sort. The butcher ends by withdrawing the blade, standing still, and letting the joy of the work sink in. He reveals the reverence that makes a live encounter possible, reverence for self and for other and for the dance of co-creation.

V. RESULTS

The fourth element of action that the woodcarver transcends and transforms is results. Perhaps the obsession with getting results deforms our action more than any other element of the active life. Too often we think of action not as an experience to be lived for its own sake but as a means to some end, and if that end is not achieved we regard the action as a failure. Furthermore, we believe that we must have the end clearly in view before the action begins and that every step in the action must be logically related to the end. Otherwise, how could we ever achieve results; how could we ever "make" things happen? But Chuang Tzu understands that the tight logic of means and ends can easily lead to banality or worse. If the woodcarver had acted this way he would never have created a bell stand of such grace.

It is easy to describe the fatal flaw in action that is rigidly oriented toward results, though acting differently is difficult. When we invest much time and energy in imaging a certain outcome, that image becomes more real for us than what is happening as we act. We become blind to the clues that action itself yields, clues to the reality of both the means and the ends, clues that call us to change course or speed or style if we want to stay in touch with what is really going on. We ignore the fact that right action is a process of birthing that cannot be forced, but only followed. Yes, we can exercise some influence over the course of the action and what comes out of it. But there is no way that we can predict outcomes, since they emerge from the intricate interplay of the actor, the other, and the setting of the action.

I feel sorry for teachers (to take one example) who are required to spell out precise "learning objectives" long before a class begins so that they can measure their own "effectiveness." I feel sorry for their students, too. Education dominated by preconceived images of what must be learned can hardly be educational. Authentic teaching and learning requires a live encounter with the unexpected, an element of suspense and surprise, an evocation of that which we did not know until it happened. If these elements are not present, we may be training or indoctrinating students, but we are not educating them. In any arena of action—rearing children, counseling people, repairing machines, writing books—right action depends on yielding our images of particular outcomes to the organic realities of ourselves, the other, and the adventure of action itself.

But this yielding requires us to confront our fears once more. Behind our obsession with projecting results and gearing our actions toward them is our need to control the other and the situation; and behind our need to control is our fear of what will happen if we lose control. If we lack confidence that life is trustworthy, that a life of live encounters will take us toward wholeness, then we will forever feel the need to manipulate, and goal setting will be one of our major strategies. But once we begin to see that life is a live encounter whether we like it or not—once we begin to understand that we can't get out of it, so we must get into it—then this concern for results will take its proper place in our active lives. Never in this world will we be free of a concern for results, but we can transcend and transform that concern the way the woodcarver did.

Our culture's fearful obsession with results has sometimes, ironically, led us to abandon great objectives and settle for trivial and mediocre ends. The reason is simple. As long as "effectiveness" is the ultimate standard by which we judge our actions, we will act only toward ends we are sure we can achieve. People who undertake projects of real breadth and depth are very unlikely to be "effective," since effectiveness is measured by short-term results (never mind the fact that such people may be creating cultural legacies by their "failures"). But people with small visions will win the effectiveness awards, since those projects are so insignificant that they can almost always "succeed" (never mind the fact that they contribute nothing of real merit to the commonweal).

When I think of the great works we are called to in our lives, works we avoid at peril of our souls, I think of works in which we cannot possibly be "effective." I mean such things as

loving other people, opposing injustice, comforting the grieving, bringing an end to war. There can be no "effectiveness"
in these tasks, only the commitment to work away at them,
and if we judge such work by the standard of measurable outcomes, the only possible result will be defeat and despair.

I remember talking with a friend who has worked for many
years at the Catholic Worker, a ministry to the poor in New
York City. Daily she tries to respond to waves of human mis-
ery that are as ceaseless as surf in that community. Out of my
deep not-knowing I asked her how she could keep doing a
work that never showed any results, a work in which the
problems keep getting worse instead of better. I will never
forget her enigmatic answer: "The thing you don't understand, Parker, is that just because something is impossible
doesn't mean you shouldn't do it!"

I have another friend who has devoted most of his adult life
to resisting the madness of war through actions of justice and
peace. He has done everything from painfully unearthing the
seeds of violence in his personal life to living in poverty so as
to stay below the taxation level. He owns nothing in his own
name because, if he did, the government could collect it as
back-taxes. The money he "should" have given the government over the years, and more, he has donated to peace and
justice projects.

Does he have any results to show for his efforts? Has he
been effective? Hardly—at least, not by the normal calculus.
His years of commitment to peacemaking have been years of
steady increase in wars and rumors of wars. So how does he
stay healthy and sane? How does he maintain a commitment
to this sort of active life? His answer completes the koan offered by my friend at the Catholic Worker: "I have never
asked myself if I was being effective, but only if I was being
faithful." He judges his action, not by the results it gets, but
by its fidelity to his own calling and identity.

Again, results are not irrelevant. We rightly care about outcomes; we have to live with them, and being accountable for

them is part of right action. But to make results the primary measure of action is a sure path to either inanity or insanity. The only standard that can guide and sustain us in action worth taking is whether the action corresponds to the reality of the situation, including the reality of our own inward nature.

The paradox, of course, is that faithful action does get results. Though my friends in the Catholic Worker and the peace movement have not achieved a just and warless world, they have certainly compelled others, including me, to search for ways we might live in faith with these visions. The results of faithful action cannot be foreseen, but they are sure to come about. For faithful action is action faithful to the nature of things, and when we act organically, our action has consequences for the organism. Surely the results will be healthier, more whole, when our action is freed from fear, from the need to control, from our idealistic fantasies, from the discouraging facts that surround us.

The woodcarver clearly wanted to co-create a bell stand, or else he would not have taken such care. But he took care to attend to reality without getting fixated on results, to the point that he was willing to risk no results whatsoever: "If I had not met this particular tree / There would have been / No bell stand at all." Of course, the woodcarver and my faithful friends never come up empty-handed, even when they do not meet the right tree. Finally, what they are crafting is not bell stands or justice or peace. They are crafting themselves. And the sort of selves they are becoming is their finest contribution to the increase of peace and justice and beauty in this world.

5. "The Angel": Action, Failure, and Suffering

I. WHERE ANGELS FEAR TO TREAD

The story at the heart of this chapter comes from Martin Buber, the great Jewish philosopher and storyteller. It reflects a world quite different than the world of Chuang Tzu. Buber wrote the story from an oral tradition that had originated with the Riziner Rabbi, one of many Hasidic teachers in eastern Europe in the eighteenth and nineteenth centuries, whose teachings reached back deep into the Talmudic period.[1]

If we are to learn from the story, we must recall the Jewish experience from which it comes and the Hasidic sensibility that colors it. From the outset Jews have had to confront suffering and holocaust, to wrestle continually with the stark question, Why? In the midst of Jewish history, Hasidism arose as a mystical affirmation of the spark of light that is always found in the heart of darkness, a spark that can ignite human hope and action even in the deadliest of times.

This story is about an angel who wanted to alleviate human suffering, an angel who tried to care. The mood and mode of his action are quite different from the woodcarver's, different in ways that will speak to people who have known less of the woodcarver's serenity and more of the angel's pain. But as we explore the story, we will also find profound commonalities between two great teachers, Buber and Chuang Tzu, who have much to teach us in both their differences and their agreements.

"The Angel and the World's Dominion"

There was a time when the Will of the Lord, Whose hand has the power to create and destroy all things, unleashed an endless tor-

rent of pain and sickness over the earth. The air grew heavy with
the moisture of tears, and a dim exhalation of sighs clouded it over.
Even the legions that surrounded God's throne were not immune
to the hovering sadness. One angel, in fact, was so deeply moved
by the sufferings he saw below, that his soul grew quite restless.
When he lifted his voice in song with the others, a note of per-
plexity sounded among the strains of pure faith; his thoughts re-
belled and contended with the Lord. He could no longer understand why death and deprivation need serve as connecting links in
the great Chain of Events. Then one day, he felt to his horror that
the eye of All-Being was piercing his own eye and uncovering the
confusion in his heart. Pulling himself together, he came before
the Lord, but when he tried to talk, his throat dried up. Neverthe-
less, the Lord called him by name and gently touched his lips.
Then the angel began to speak. He begged God to place the administration of the earth in his hands for a year's time, that he
might lead it to an era of well-being. The angelic bands trembled
at this audacity. But at that same moment Heaven grew bright
with the radiance of God's smile. He looked at the suppliant with
great love, as He announced His agreement. When the angel stood
up again, he too was shining.

And so a year of joy and sweetness visited the earth. The shining
angel poured the great profusion of his merciful heart over the most
anguished of her children, on those who were benumbed and terri-
fied by want. The groans of the sick and dying were no longer
heard in the land. The angel's companion in the steely armor, who
only a short time before had been rushing and roaring through the
air, stepped aside now, waiting peevishly with lowered sword, relieved of his official duties. The earth floated through a fecund sky
that left her with the burden of new vegetation. When summer was
at its height, people moved singing through the full, yellow fields;
never had such abundance existed in living memory. At harvest
time, it seemed likely that the walls would burst or the roofs fly off,
if they were going to find room to store their crops.

Proud and contented, the shining angel basked in his own glory.
For by the time the first snow of winter covered the valleys, and dominion over the earth reverted into God's hands, he had parcelled
out such an enormous bounty that the people of earth would surely
be enjoying his gifts for many years to come.

But one cold day, late in the year, a multitude of voices rose heavenwards in a great cry of anguish. Frightened by the sound, the angel journeyed down to earth and, dressed as a pilgrim, entered the first house along the way. The people there, having threshed the grain and ground it into flour, had then started baking bread—but, alas, when they took the bread out of the oven it fell to pieces and the pieces were unpalatable; they filled the mouth with a disgusting taste, like clay. And this was precisely what the angel found in the second house and in the third and everywhere he set foot. People were lying on the floor, tearing their hair and cursing the Lord of the World, who had deceived their miserable hearts with His false blessing.

The angel flew away and collapsed at God's feet. Lord, he cried, help me to understand where my power and judgment were lacking.

Then God raised his voice and spoke: Behold a truth which is known to me from the beginning of time, a truth too deep and dreadful for your delicate, generous hands, my sweet apprentice—it is this, that the earth must be nourished with decay and covered with shadows that its seeds may bring forth—and it is this, that souls must be made fertile with flood and sorrow, that through them the Great Work may be born.[2]

When I ask people whether the angel reminds them of anyone, they often name themselves. We know what it is to be filled with distress and indignation over an obvious evil, to be driven by a desire to do good, to want desperately to save someone or something, to right a terrible wrong. But many of us know, too, what it is like when our angelic intentions turn out to have unexpected and even demonic results. The angel in this story is an easily identifiable type who, depending on one's viewpoint, is either the hope of the earth or the bane of our existence—or both.

Some people say that the angel is a courageous and compassionate character who saw suffering, identified with it, and had the heart to try to do something about it. For them, the angel represents the human capacity to envision a better world against all evidence, to work for the common good against all odds. But other people see the angel as driven by ego, pride, the need for power. They see arrogance in the angel's desire to play the role of God, childishness in the angel's inability to understand the logic and limits of life. Both camps, I suspect, are projecting on the angel feelings about themselves and are revealing the deep ambivalence of hope and despair that many of us have about any effort to make the world a better place.

The fact is, of course, that we and the angel are all of the above. Our action is often a mixture of ego and innocence, and we will not become whole until we can embrace that simple fact. If we wait for purity of motive, we will never act, or our action will be immaterial. If we abandon hope for a "second innocence," our action will merely multiply cynicism. Clearly the angel was an innocent; he thought he could do away with human suffering altogether. Clearly the angel was prideful as well; he believed that he could do better than God, and he enjoyed basking "in his own glory." But many of us are like that, so we have much to learn from an angel who had both the innocence and the pride to act in the midst of his own mixed motives.

In fact, our mixed motives run deeper than innocence and pride. Our most constructive impulse is often accompanied by a destructive impulse, made all the more destructive by the fact that we usually remain oblivious to this sinister energy within us. Buber's story says that at the height of the angel's glory, when all seemed well on earth, "The angel's companion in the steely armor, who only a short time before had been rushing and roaring through the air, stepped aside now, waiting peevishly with lowered sword, relieved of his official duties." This, I suspect, is the angel's destructive alter ego, his shadow, a force that can be held off for a while, but that will assert itself all the more vigorously the longer it is pushed aside. Had the angel better understood his companion in steely armor, his angelic actions might have had a less violent outcome.

I am reminded of the wisdom of Stanley Vishnewski, a man of great heart who gave himself to the poorest of the poor through the Catholic Worker, that communal ministry in New York's Bowery. Stanley, who spent his whole adult life in works of charity, was fond of saying that the Catholic Worker community was made up of saints and martyrs: "The saints create the martyrs and the martyrs create the saints!" He understood the inevitable duality of individuals and communities who set out to do good.[3]

In the midst of this duality, it is important to see that the angel is not the same at the end of the story as he is at the beginning. Duality does not mean a permanent split within us. Duality is dynamic, and its tensions can help us grow. The angel grows as the tale moves along; we see an evolution of character that is not just an artifact of the story but a fact of life. As we act, the real action is often not what we are doing to the world around us but what we are doing to ourselves. Every action involves self-transformation, and we will learn the most from this story if we watch what happens to the angel's character as the action proceeds.

Though some people see the angel as being compassionate from the outset of the tale, I do not. Compassion means, literally, the capacity to be with the suffering of another. Though the angel was "deeply moved" by human suffering at the beginning of the story, the text says that he was moved only by "the sufferings he saw below." His relation to that suffering was both visual and vertical: he *saw* it rather than touched it, and he kept himself *above* it rather than entering into it.

Only later in the story—and then only under great duress—does the angel make the descent toward common ground that is the movement of true compassion when he "journeyed down to earth." But at the outset, the tale says, he simply "poured the great profusion of his merciful heart over the most anguished of [earth's] children." Pouring is an act that can be done only from above.

That is always our temptation when we set out to do good—to do it in a way that leaves us above the fray. But our desire to stay above it all reveals our misunderstanding of right action. Action that distances us from "the other" can never be right; we cannot do good by standing back and pulling levers that drop bounty on people who need it. Right action can be only an immersion of ourselves in reality, an immersion that involves us in relationship, that takes us to our place in the organic nature of things.

Remember the woodcarver. By emptying himself through fasting, he found his right relationship to the world of the prince and the people, of the forest and the tree. By interacting with that organic reality the woodcarver was able to co-create a work of beauty. But the angel, who stays up in heaven, is unavailable for relationship with the suffering people on earth and with earth's own cycle of growth. The fact that he means well and has deep feeling for those who suffer does not alter the fact that his action is far removed from those he would serve. It cannot possibly be right action because at such a distance the actor can have no clue to what reality requires.

To suffer with another person does not mean to drown oneself in the other's suffering; that would be as foolish as jumping in the pool to save a sinking swimmer only to drown oneself. More to the point, I doubt that it is even possible to enter fully into another person's pain, for suffering is a profoundly solitary experience. To suffer with another person means to be there in whatever way possible, to share the circumstances of the other's life as much as one can—not to add to the world's pool of suffering, but to gain intimate understanding of what the other requires.

What we usually learn, once we are there, is that there is no "fix" for the person who suffers, only the slow and painful process of walking through the suffering to whatever lies on the other side. Once there, we learn that being there is the best we can do, being there not as cure but as companion to the person who suffers on his or her slow journey. There is no arm's-length "solution" for suffering, and people who offer such only add to the pain. But there is comfort and even healing in the presence of people who know how to be with others, how to be fully there.

Twice in my life I have experienced deep depression. Both times various friends tried to rescue me with well-intended encouragement and advice: "Get outside and enjoy the sunshine," or "You have such a good life—why be depressed?" or "I know a book that might really help you." For all their good intentions, these friends made me even more depressed. They did not understand what I was going through, did not understand that there was no easy "fix." Their advice served only to distance them from me, leaving me even more isolated.

In fact, distancing ourselves from each other's pain is the hidden agenda behind most of our efforts to "fix" each other with advice. If you take my advice, and do it right, you will get well and I will be off the hook. But if you do not follow my advice, or do not follow it properly, I am off the hook nonetheless: I have done the best I could, and your continued suffering is clearly your fault. By trying to fix you with advice, rather than simply suffering with you, I hold myself away from your pain.

In the midst of my depression I had a friend who took a different tack. Every afternoon at around four o'clock he came to me, sat me in a chair, removed my shoes, and massaged my feet. He hardly said a word, but he was there, he was with me. He was a lifeline for me, a link to the human community and thus to my own humanity. He had no need to "fix" me. He knew the meaning of compassion.

The angel does not understand compassion at the start of this story—or, if he does, he is afraid to act on his knowledge. Instead, he asks God to make him the earth's chief executive officer for a year, to place him at the apex of the cosmic organizational chart so that he can fix all earthly ills from that detached vantage point. If the angel had proceeded differently—if he had asked at the outset to become a pilgrim on earth so that he could share the plight of the people—he would never have planted the seeds of false hope that grew into false wheat and were baked into false bread. It may be easier to act from a distance than to practice true compassion, but such action rarely results in anyone being fed.

II. THE HEALING POWER OF FAILURE

Early in the story, the angel merely "sees" suffering from above and is "moved" by it. Then he asks and receives from God the power to try to relieve that suffering, a power that he exercises from on high by "pouring" goodness down onto earth. But his action fails because it is not organic, not true to the nature of things. Just when the people on earth should be enjoying the fruits of the angel's bounty, "a multitude of voices rose heavenwards in a great cry of anguish" and the angel was "frightened by the sound."

This is a crucial juncture in the story, the point at which the angel turns from detached do-gooding toward the beginnings of true compassion. There are three important elements in his turning. The first is the fact that he moves from seeing suffering to hearing it. We know how detached the act of seeing can be, since we continually see things on TV that may touch us but do not alter our lives. We watch scenes of cruelty and carnage while the newscaster's sophisticated voice-over distances us from reality by putting everything "in perspective." Were we to hear, really hear, the sound of warfare, the screams and the groans of the dying, we might be more deeply engaged.

A second important element in the angel's turning is that, while he is "moved" by the suffering he sees at the outset of the story, he is "frightened" when he hears the cries of anguish that later rise from earth to heaven. As important as it is to be moved, that experience can be maudlin and sentimental, a substitute for real emotion. How many of us are moved at Christmas by the plight of the hungry and the homeless, only to forget them the rest of the year? To be frightened, however, is something else. We feel fear when our own being is at stake, when we sense our implication in the plight of others. Fear is a real emotion that may lead us to true compassion, because in our fear we ourselves are suffering.

Why does the angel feel afraid when he hears the cries of anguish that arise after his year of playing God? Because those cries are the first clue that he may have failed at what he had tried to do—and failure is the third and crucial element in the angel's turning toward compassion. Compassion begins when the angel allows himself to suffer the fact that his well-intended acts have added to the pain of the people, allows himself to suffer from the failure caused by his own insensitivity and ineptitude. Only when he realizes that he may have failed does the angel begin his all-important downward movement toward earth.

If downward movement is key to our quest for reality, then failure is key to our growth. Success, or the illusion of success, is an upward movement, an inflation of the ego that makes us lighter than air. But failure is life's ballast. It restrains our tendency to float away on a bloated ego and pulls us back toward common ground. The angel floats in heaven until he fails, and his failure brings him down to earth. Failure is the angel's mode of contemplation, his way of falling from illusion toward reality.

But it is not failure alone that brings the angel down and moves him toward compassion. It is his willingness to confront, acknowledge, and explore his failure. He could have ignored it altogether. He could have glanced at it and tried to palm if off on someone else—on those ungrateful people, or on that cruel God. But the angel claims the failure as his own and allows it to hollow out his heart: "The angel flew away and collapsed at God's feet. Lord, he cried, help me to understand where my power and judgment were lacking." Learning from failure is not a cool and calculated act. It tears at the heart and opens us against our will.

Several years ago I was asked to consult with a wealthy, white suburban church that had "yoked" itself with a poor black congregation in the inner city. The suburbanites, most of them professional people, believed that the relation of the two churches had been worked out with great care. But now, three years later, they were frustrated by the fact that their sister congregation was not making good use, or even any use, of the financial and human resources that the suburbanites had pledged to provide. They suspected that the problem was due to differences between black and white culture, and they wanted me, as a sociologist, to help them understand and negotiate those differences.

But, with the story of the angel very much in mind, I did not want to take a sociological approach to the problem. In fact, I did not view the situation as a problem to be solved. Instead, I suggested that in a congregation as wealthy as theirs, among people with so much power, the one kind of poverty that they could experience was the poverty of being unable to achieve the results they wanted. Their frustration with their sister church was, perhaps, as close as they would ever get to the daily poverty of inner city blacks who can achieve so few of their cherished goals. My suggestion to the white suburbanites was not to "solve" the problem through sociological analysis, but to immerse themselves as deeply as they could in their own failure, to see if they could draw nearer in compassion to their downtown brothers and sisters.

Though the story of the angel ends too soon to tell, perhaps the angel is embarked on this same course when he collapses at God's feet and cries, ". . . help me to understand where my power and judgment were lacking." His is not a problem to be solved, but a truth to be lived, the truth that our highest hopes often die aborning. As the story ends, the angel has the same choice that we have: to allow the limits of life to diminish and embitter us, or to embrace those limits in ways that expand and illumine our lives.

The angel prays "help me to understand where my power and judgment were lacking," and his life depends on how he understands the answer God gives. A false understanding would make the angel feel like a guilty fool who should never try such a dumb trick again, and who would do well to hide out for the rest of his life. A true understanding would allow the angel to face his own foolishness, but to know that he had been a fool for love, that his mistake was a mistake of the heart. While the angel needs to let his failure teach his heart a thing or two, he need never withhold his heart from love.

Our culture puts such a premium on success, and such sanctions on failure, that we find it hard to affirm the rightness of failing at a good cause, to affirm the creativity that failure can contain. Most of us still treat failure as terminal, just as we were taught in school, where an *F* in a course was a final verdict from which there was no appeal. It seems to make no difference to us that science, as I have said, learns as much from failure as from success; that the most creative modern businesses encourage their employees to risk failure for the sake of what they might learn; that generative people fail frequently.

The paradox is that failure may turn to growth, while success can turn to self-satisfaction and closure. This merely echoes Jesus' famous saying that if you seek your life you will lose it, but if you lose your life you will find it (see Matthew 16:25). No matter how many times we see proof of this paradox, we find it hard to act accordingly, to invite failure and the "losing" of our lives. In fact, I think that Jesus spoke those words, not so much to advise us how to act, but simply to "tell it like it is." Seldom will we be willing to lose and fail on purpose, confident that our loss will be translated into gain. But even if we do not live this way intentionally, the paradox will happen in our lives. The only question is whether we will recognize and receive the transformation when it comes.

Our receptiveness will be the greater if we can do what the angel did. At his moment of failure and defeat, he did not try to cover up, to stonewall, to make excuses, to put on a good face. Instead, he allowed himself to feel the abject humiliation of it all. He collapsed, he cried, he admitted his ignorance, he begged for help. Rather than holding his failure at arm's length and trying to move on, he entered fully into the pain of it and sought help from the only source left. That is all we can do when we fail so miserably—but if we do it, it is enough.

III. WHAT KIND OF GOD IS THIS?

The source from which the angel finally seeks help is a God who, as portrayed in the story, makes some people angry. "What kind of God is this," they ask, "who would set the angel up for such a terrible fall just to learn a lesson, and who would let the earth suffer just so the angel could learn?" Some people say that this is not the God they know, while others say it is a God they have known and rejected. In either case they despise Buber's God, a God who seems to hold all the cards, and hold them close to the vest, in a game that is unnecessarily cruel.

I have no need to attack or defend this God. But by exploring the way God works in this story, and our own response to it, we have a chance to explore our own sense of ultimate reality. What is the deep context of our action? What kind of cosmic stuff do we think our lives are embedded in, and how does it shape what we do? Our own sense of reality may be revealed and stretched by reflecting on the God of Buber's tale.

Some people say that this God merely gives the angel the gift of freedom that God gives all of us in real life, the freedom to do good or to make costly and grievous mistakes. They say that they treasure their freedom, and love God for giving it, even when it issues in tragedy, because the greater tragedy would be not to be free. But God's critics are not so easily satisfied. They point to the fact that God, at the end of the story, says he is letting the angel in on a secret that God knew all along, a secret that had doomed the angel's best efforts before he had ever begun, the secret that you cannot have life without death. "If God knew this all along," the critics ask, "why did God not have the decency to tell the angel before giving him all that power? God could have saved the angel, to say nothing of the people, a great deal of trouble by doing so."

But that critique of God's behavior misses some crucial points. The story tells us that the angel, from the very beginning, knows the truth that God tells him at the end. Early on, the narrative says that the angel "could no longer understand why death and deprivation need serve as connecting links in the great Chain of Events," which is no different from the truth that God announces to the angel at the end of the tale. The problem from the beginning is that the angel *knew* the truth but "could no longer *understand*" it. That is, he refused to accept what he already knew.

Some of us do a lot of that, I think. We know things that we do not want to accept, and so we act as if we do not know them—until our actions and their outcomes force us to acknowledge what we already knew. This is the learning cycle of contemplation-and-action, the continuing struggle between illusion and reality. It is not a fictional device, but a fact of real life that the angel at the end of the story is forced by his own actions to recall a truth he already knew when the tale began.

It seems possible to me that the people on earth also refused to accept what they inwardly knew (though I say this on the evidence of personal experience, not of the story itself). During the time of the angel's administration, when earth knew nothing but abundance and joy, some people must have sensed the unreality of it all, must have feared that this abundance was the false blessing it turned out to be. But no one protested. We are often ready to receive a false blessing no matter what the eventual cost; it takes unusual maturity to turn one down. Wishful recipients are as guilty as deceitful givers when false blessings are handed out in politics, in religion, in personal life.

So Buber's God might be acquitted of irresponsibility on at least two counts. One, God gave the angel freedom, even to mess up. Two, even if God had reminded the angel at the outset that life demands suffering, the angel still would have tried to circumvent that truth. But those understandings of God do not go deep enough. The truth about God in this story—and, I believe, about God in our lives—is far more radical and unsettling: God is in this mess with us and has the same unfulfilled yearnings that make our human hearts ache.

If reality is a continual process of co-creation between ourselves and God, as I believe it is, then God is not a fixed quantity in some cosmic equation. Instead, God experiments, succeeds, fails, changes, learns, suffers, enjoys, and grows— just as we do. Buber's story does not describe a divine set-up, intended to teach the naive angel a tough lesson at the expense of humankind. Instead, it describes a God who yearns for a better world, who pushes against the limits of things, who needs us as companions in this pushing, and who gets lonely when we do not respond.

Of course, I am now describing a God who, in pushing against the limits of things, is pushing against part of God's own self. The God of this story has the same inner paradox that the angel and we ourselves have, as the very first line makes clear: "There was a time when the Will of the Lord, Whose hand has the power to create and destroy all things, unleashed an endless torrent of pain and sickness over the earth."

Some of us are distressed by such a description of God. We prefer the popular image of a God who is wholly creative, who struggles valiantly against the alien powers of destruction that the universe "mistakenly" contains. But simple observation tells us that reality requires both building up and tearing down. If God is ultimate reality, then God surely must embody the paradox of destruction and creativity. By ac-

knowledging this paradox in God, we are better able to penetrate the common illusion of our own "niceness," better able
to touch the complex reality of our own nature and of the nature in which we are embedded. At the heart of reality, we
and God together are stretched by the creative tension between death and life, finding ourselves tugged sometimes this
way, sometimes that.

In Buber's story, though God "unleashed" death on the
world, God also yearns for new life and hopes that the angel
can counteract the destruction. That interpretation is based in
part on the fact that the angel's action does not begin with his
own feeling of being "deeply moved by the sufferings he saw
below." Instead, it begins when "the eye of All-Being was
piercing his own eye and uncovering the confusion in his
heart." The angel has deep feelings about the suffering he
sees, but they remain inarticulate until God pierces his heart
and moves the angel from feeling to action. God does not
wait passively for the angel to act; God clearly wants the angel to do something, so God intervenes in the angel's inner
struggle and frees the angel from his paralysis.

At that moment, the story says, the angel "felt . . . horror."
Well he should have, for he had been pierced by divine love.
"Love in action is a harsh and dreadful thing," said Dos-
toyevski. When God's love for the world pierces our armor of
fear, as it did the angel's, it is an awesome experience of calling and accountability.

When the angel finally "pulled himself together" and
"came before the Lord," he was unable to utter a word, for
his throat was too dry. Again God intervenes, calling the angel by name and gently touching his lips, enabling him to
speak. Finally, the angel is able to respond to the call. He begs
God to give him power over the earth for one year, a petition
that has the angelic bands trembling at the angel's audacity.
"But at that same moment Heaven grew bright with the radiance of God's smile. He looked at the suppliant with great
love, as He announced His agreement."

I find no hint of cynicism in those words, no suggestion that God is setting the innocent angel up for a lesson. I find only the evidence of love, the love that God must feel for those who are willing to risk pushing the boundaries of things as they are. At this point in the story I think that even God has suspended belief in the iron-clad law of suffering; at this point God hopes against hope that the angel might make a difference. God's immense love for the angel is the love that God has for anyone willing to risk failure so that life might be lived more fully, more whole.

Another key to this interpretation is in the simple fact that God gives the angel power to do what he wants to do. Here is one of the great acts of love, empowering another person, knowing full well that the person will probably make serious mistakes with that power, knowing that those mistakes may be costly even to the one who does the empowering. If there is a parent-child motif in God's relation to the angel, it is not that of the manipulative parent setting out to teach the child a lesson, with predictable outcomes. Instead, God in this story is a trusting and risking parent who gives the child the power and freedom to live his or her life to the fullest, no matter what. Any parent knows that this is at once the most painful and the most rewarding gift one can give. A child may misuse his or her power, but neither we nor our children can be fully human if we do not empower them to live life by their own best lights.

At the end of the story, after the angel has failed and fallen, God speaks hard truth to him. But in that speech I sense nothing of "I told you so." Instead, God's words are delivered with an air of resignation, an acknowledgment that the universe has laws that seem immutable, that God as well as the angel needs to recall this deep truth. Even so, in that speech I hear God's infinite yearning for an increase of goodness, God's infinite willingness to suffer and try again, to grieve and begin once more.

IV. THE GREAT WORK TO BE BORN

The teaching that God gives the angel at the end of the story concludes with a tantalizing reference to a "Great Work" that is to be born through "souls . . . made fertile with flood and sorrow." The phrase is easy to pass by, coming as it does in a final flurry of rhetoric. But much of the meaning of the story depends on what we take this "Great Work" to be and how we understand our relation to it.

On one level, the lesson God has to teach is simply the truth about nature itself: Seeds do not grow if they are not "nourished with decay." That is what composting and fertilizing are all about. By ridding earth of decay for a year, the angel destroyed the conditions that allow true grain to grow, and the result was grain that could not nourish people once it was made into bread. This law of nature, God tells the angel, is the law of human nature as well. Decay and shadow, flood and sorrow, must fertilize souls as well as seeds if the fruit of our inner life is to nourish us and others.

But God's teaching has a more immediate, less abstract, meaning. With it, God is trying to help the angel understand the very process that God and the angel are going through. The Great Work is the work the angel is engaged in—the work of developing compassion by suffering the fires of failure. God is engaged in this Great Work with us, continually expanding the scope of God's own compassion by experiencing the failures of love.

If my interpretation of the God in this story seems heretical, I apologize in advance for taking it one step further. I believe that the interpretation I have offered—in which God sends a compassionate creature into the breach, desperately hoping that the creature can break the rules of life and make something new and better happen—is not unlike the biblical story of Jesus' birth and life and mission. According to Christian tradition, God sent Jesus down to earth as a human incarnation of divine compassion. His mission was to challenge, and break, one of the elemental rules of the universe, the rule that allows death always to have the last word. The angel in Buber's story could be seen as a prototype of Jesus, and not surprisingly so, for the Jesus of history arose exactly in the context of Jewish hopes for a Messiah who could break the rules.

Still a key question remains. In the case of Jesus, did God know the outcome in advance? If so, I am probably a heretic for suggesting that Buber's God, and mine, continually hopes against hope that something new might happen in this suffering world. But if the God of Jesus knew the outcome in advance, knew that Jesus would break the bonds of death through resurrection; and if Jesus is this self-same God incarnate, holding this same certainty; then why so much *Sturm und Drang* in the Gospel story? Why, if God and Jesus could predict the denouement, does Jesus suffer and doubt and sweat and cry out that he has been forsaken, when his moment of death arrives? The human side of the Gospel story makes sense only if this God is a participant in the struggle with us, a God who, like Jesus, is uncertain of the outcome, but still willing to take risky actions of love. Otherwise, Jesus is simply play-acting in a theatrical production whose conclusion is never in doubt, and a play-acting Jesus is not a helpful companion on the human journey with its very real doubts and fears.

Some Christians have reacted with anger and even violence to the filmed version of Kazantzakis's *Last Temptation of Christ,* a novel that explores the human emotions that Jesus might have struggled with.[4] Apparently, these Christians find the humanness of Jesus offensive, despite the church's insistence that Jesus was as fully human as he was divine. But the point that I want to make may be more offensive still: God is not all-knowing and all-powerful. God depends on partnerships with various beings to accomplish the Great Work here on earth. Jesus, it seems to me, is a prime example of such a partnership.

I find a profound flaw in the image of a God who has set everything up, past and present and future; who knows exactly what has been and is and will be; who has absolute power to control and change any of this; but who simply lets the script play itself out into eternity. In part, such a God is boring, quite unlike the God I experience. But the deeper flaw is that I cannot love such a God—nor can I feel that such a God loves me. Love is a dynamic relationship, a two-way exchange of energy. When God is conceived as an omniscient and omnipotent Prime Mover, no such energy is generated. Entropy ensues, the universe becomes a cold and empty place, and the Great Work will never be done.

Entropy seems common in religious life today. Perhaps it is because we are too often taught to worship a God whom we need but who does not need us, who is said to love us but who is too powerful for us to love. Only a God who is vulnerable and even needy will evoke our love in a way that completes the circuit of human-and-divine, the circuit in which each of us becomes a carrier of love's energy, a co-creator of the Great Work to be born. Whenever that circuit is completed, we are jolted out of our illusion of isolation and into the knowledge that we can find right action only in relationship, in communion, in community.

The angel's arrogance and pride is found not only in his confidence that he could do things better than God but that he could do it all alone. He asks no help from anyone—from God, from fellow angels, from the people on earth. He asks only for complete executive power, on the assumption that if *he* were at the top of the hierarchy all would be well. But that assumption massively misses the point. The problem of suffering that concerns the angel can never be solved by executive decree; in fact, suffering can never be solved. It can only be shared in compassion, shared in community, and every effort to put ourselves in charge of the relief effort weakens the very sharing in which our hope resides.

Whatever else the Great Work may be, it surely will be a

work of community. That is simply another way of saying that the angel can be understood as a prototypical Christ, for the "body of Christ" so central to Christian understanding is itself an image of community. The angel is a broken being at the end of Buber's tale, but he is broken open to the possibility of community. He knows now that he is not self-sufficient, and in that knowledge he has a chance to discover the centrality of relationship—to God, to others, to his several inner selves. If he takes that chance, if he realizes the possibility of community in his own life, his failure will have been transformed, and he will become a compassionate being "with healing in his wings" (Mal. 4:2, JB).

The marvelous thing about learning from a story is that a story never ends, so our learning from it need not end either. Buber brings his story to a temporary close, with God delivering a great truth to the angel. But what happens next? Does the angel slink off in humiliation and try to hide his face? Does he have a sudden illumination, realizing that his failure contains vital learnings that can empower him to take the next step? Does he shout back at God with anger, accusing God of failures larger than his own? There are a thousand possibilities—and whichever one we choose, it will teach us a great deal about ourselves and our view of reality.

My own extension of the story goes something like this. The angel, having listened to God explain the necessity of suffering, asks God if it ever gets lonely to live in the midst of such difficult truths, surrounded by folks who refuse either to embrace them or to challenge them. God admits that being God is no picnic, that God has a great yearning for companionship and community. The angel, who now knows exactly how loneliness feels, experiences a rush of compassion for God. The angel and God confess their need for each other, and their need for as many companions as they can find, and they come together in a communion that is the rebirth of the Messiah on earth.

Were that to happen, in story or in fact, it would not be the first time, nor would it be the last.

6. "Jesus in the Desert": The Temptations of Action

I. THE DESERT EXPERIENCE

In this chapter and the next I explore two stories that are more familiar to many of us than the tales of Buber and Chuang Tzu—and our familiarity may pose problems. These are stories from the Christian Scriptures that some of us have been hearing all our lives. They have been interpreted for us so often that our minds may be closed to new meanings or, if our minds are closed to the church altogether, we may not believe that the stories have any meaning at all. The fact that Jesus is the central figure in these tales may be a stumbling block for some people. His name may conjure up either a sacred relic to be protected from insight at all costs, or a discredited worldview preserved mainly by the ignorant for the sake of false comfort.

I have no way to authenticate these stories for people who are either alienated from Christian tradition or committed to an inflexible version of it. But if we cannot interact with these stories about Jesus in the same freedom that we bring to stories about woodcarvers and angels, our loss is great, for they are great stories. As we approach these Jesus tales we need somehow to preserve the freshness, the sense of strangeness, the mix of intrigue and incredulity with which we instinctively approach Taoist and Hasidic tales.

Christians need to let the Jesus of these stories be a person in the midst of dramatic action, rather than a robot programmed to prove some theological point again and again.

People who reject Christianity need to give Jesus his humanity as well. If we can suspend our need to defend or demolish this ideology or that, we will find in these stories a mother lode of insight as rich as can be found in any other tale told by people earnestly seeking truth.

"The Temptations of Jesus"

Filled with the Holy Spirit, Jesus left the Jordan and was led by the Spirit through the wilderness, being tempted there by the devil for forty days. During that time he ate nothing and at the end he was hungry. Then the devil said to him, "If you are the Chosen One, tell this stone to turn into a loaf." But Jesus replied, "Scripture says: 'People do not live on bread alone.' "

Then leading him to a height, the devil showed him in a moment of time all the kingdoms of the world and said to him, "I will give you all this power and the glory of these kingdoms, for it has been committed to me and I give it to anyone I choose. Worship me, then, and it shall all be yours." But Jesus answered him, "Scripture says: 'You must worship the Lord your God, and serve God alone.' "

Then he led him to Jerusalem and made him stand on the parapet of the Temple. "If you are the Chosen One," he said to him, "throw yourself down from here, for Scripture says: 'God will put angels in charge of you to guard you,' and again: 'They will hold you up on their hands in case you hurt your foot against a stone.' " But Jesus answered him, "It has been said: 'You must not put the Lord your God to the test.' "

Having exhausted all these ways of tempting him, the devil left him, to return at the appointed time.

Jesus, with the power of the Spirit in him, returned to Galilee; and his reputation spread throughout the countryside. He taught in their synagogues and everyone praised him. (Luke 4:1–15, JB).*

As we begin our journey into this strange tale, we need to note its location in Luke's overall account of Jesus' life. In the chapters before this one, Luke tells of Jesus' birth and the events surrounding it and gives a quick recounting of what

---

* Text slightly altered for the sake of inclusive language.

little he knows of Jesus' first thirty years. In the chapters after this one, Luke tells story after story of Jesus in action: Jesus preaching, Jesus confronting, Jesus healing, Jesus dying. So this brief telling of Jesus' temptations in the desert comes at that pivotal point where he is emerging from the hiddenness of private life into the glare of public life, turning from anonymity toward the notoriety of world-historical action.

This placement of the narrative of Jesus' temptations is no accident. It reflects the craft of a master storyteller, the genius of a classical myth. The temptations are portrayed as the portal through which Jesus must pass to gain access to the world of right action, the crucible in which he is refined so that he can undertake an active life that is not, in the words of Chuang Tzu, "a pity." Where Buber's story ends with the angel confronting a great test, Luke's story of Jesus' active life begins with a testing—and the way Jesus responds to it makes all the rest of the Jesus tales possible. We have much to learn from Jesus' encounter with the devil on the threshold of Jesus' active life.

Because the story is compressed into roughly a dozen sentences, it is easy to imagine that the temptations themselves came and went quickly, in no more time than it takes for Jesus and the devil to conduct their repartee. But that would be a mistake because it robs Jesus of his humanity, as if he could dismiss the devil with such debonair ease! The story tells us that Jesus was in the wilderness "being tempted there by the devil for forty days." Of course, in the Scriptures, forty is the number of days it rained during the great flood and the number of years Israel wandered in the wilderness. It is a figure used simply to represent "a long period of time."[1]

So Jesus wrestled with these temptations for a considerable period, time and time again. His wrestling was not the sort we see on TV, scripted and staged, but a sweat-and-blood encounter, as risky and uncertain of outcome as life itself. In fact, at the end of the story, after Jesus has gone to heroic lengths to defeat the devil, we are told that his struggle is not over: "Having exhausted all these ways of tempting him, the devil left him, to return at the appointed time." The story suggests that temptation never ends, that the threshold test for right action must be passed again and again. We do both Jesus and ourselves a disservice if we reduce his agony to a few lines of snappy dialogue.

To understand the story, we need to note how Jesus got into the desert in the first place—into this lonely and heartbreaking place where he was to face the hardest challenge he had yet known. Surely it was the devil who took him there. But the story says that Jesus "was led by the Spirit through the wilderness, being tempted there by the devil for forty days." How odd that God should seem almost in league with the powers of darkness in Luke's rendering of this tale.

That, of course, is exactly how things work at these deep levels of life. In the midst of depression I once asked my spiritual director how I could be feeling such despair when not long before the depression hit I had been feeling so close to God? "Simple," she said. "The closer you get to light, the closer you get to darkness." The deepest things in life come not singly but in paradoxical pairs, where the light and the dark intermingle. The temptations story makes it clear that God's Spirit is not safe but dangerous, that those who act on the Spirit's urging will sometimes find themselves hungry and thirsty and filled with fear.

If talk of *the Spirit* works for some of us, we tend to choke on *the devil*. It is as hard for us to take seriously the image of a horned and caped personification of evil as it is for us to abide the image of God as an old man with a beard. The popular song that says, "The devil made me do it the first time—the second time I done it on my own," simply shows that the devil may be good for a laugh these days, but not for much else.[2]

But perhaps we still speak of the devil; we simply do it in a language less jarring to modern ears. We may no longer say that a person is possessed by Satan, but we readily say that he or she is power-hungry or has a character disorder. We may no longer say that a society is under the sway of the Evil One, but we readily speak of institutional racism or sexism. If we can understand how we are "tempted" by these psychological and social conditions, if we can translate archaic devil-talk into contemporary terms for the same evils and ills, we may be able to enter more deeply into the story of Jesus' temptations in the desert.

We might enter still more deeply through a leap of imagination. I am intrigued by the biblical idea that the devil is "an angel put out of heaven because of his rebellion against God and his desire to presume the prerogatives of divinity . . . . "[3] That notion links this story of Jesus with Buber's tale of the angel who wanted divine power over the earth, and it sharpens the question of what Buber's angel learned by failing. Is the devil in this biblical story an angel who tried to set things right but refused to learn from his failure? Is this devil still trying to set things right by finding an ally who is willing to risk the same mistake? Let us keep these questions alive while we explore the temptations that Jesus faced as he embarked on his active life.

II. TURN THIS STONE TO BREAD

As we begin this exploration, we need first to understand the nature of *temptations*. That word is often a negative one for us, suggesting traps that are put in our path to snare us, pits we may fall into if we are not extremely careful. The conventional wisdom is that temptations are to be avoided at all costs, and if we do not avoid them, we will find ourselves locked in mortal combat that could lead to the loss of our immortal souls.

But the word *temptation* has an instructive root: the Latin *temptare,* meaning to touch, to try or test, to feel experimentally. Deep in the word itself is the truth that we must act out some things to discover who we are in relation to them. Some of these traps and snares may actually be opportunities for experiential learning, that profound source of knowledge that many of us need in order to grow. Perhaps the path of action is riddled not with deadly pits but with chances to touch, to try, to test. Whether we walk that path, and how we walk it, depends on how we understand its temptations.

As I write these hopeful words about temptations I hear the old saw, "If you think it's poison, you don't drink it to make sure." But there are other old saws, such as, "One person's meat is another person's poison." And we also have the pointed words of André Maurois: "There are certain persons for whom pure Truth is poison."[4]

If we are to experience the story of Jesus in the desert as anything other than a boringly predictable morality play, we must be open to the educative potentials of temptations, to the fact that temptations are not merely there to be avoided. I refer again to that ancient theologian who saw not just "sin" but "happy sin" in the fact that Adam and Eve succumbed to temptation in the Garden of Eden, thus bequeathing us the rich legacy of human consciousness and history. That legacy poses us with problems, but the fact that we are conscious co-creators of the human experience is a pearl of great price. If the temptation is put before you, and you flunk the test, as Adam and Eve did, it may not be a terminal failure at all. It may be the opening of a great and generative journey into truth.

In the first temptation Jesus faces, the devil says, "If you are the Chosen One, tell this stone to turn into a loaf." But Jesus refuses him. "Scripture says: 'People do not live on bread alone.' " Ironically, this quotation has caused some Christians to succumb to a sin that the devil himself must applaud, the sin of *spiritualizing* basic human needs to the point of ignoring poverty and starvation. These Christians have been deluded into thinking that Jesus' words justify the attempt to "save the souls" of the starving without feeding them, to address the "spiritual" needs of the poor without putting food in their mouths and without challenging the injustice that deprives them of their fair share.

But these words of Jesus, his refusal to turn bread into stone, are his response to the devil, not to starving people. Once Jesus moves through these temptations and embarks on his public ministry, he works a number of "miracles," including the provision of bread for people who are hungry. What Jesus says and does is related to context, and when the circumstances are right he has no inhibitions about using his powers to meet authentic needs. We need only to understand why the circumstances in this story were wrong.

The devil prefaces his challenge to turn bread into stone with a taunt that takes a very familiar form: "If you are the Chosen One . . . " Though few of us get needled for thinking we are Chosen, the tone of that taunt should remind us of outward or inward voices in our lives: "If you are so able . . . ," "If you are a real woman or man . . . ," "If you truly care . . . ," "If you are such a good parent . . . " The root temptation here is almost irresistible. It is not the temptation to do a magic trick, which most of us know we cannot. It is the temptation to prove our identity, which many of us feel we must.

The temptation must have been especially intense in Jesus' case. After all, the coming of the Chosen One, of the Messiah, was a long-expected event in the history of Israel. In Jesus' time, and prior to it, the Hebrew people had seen and rejected many pretenders to the throne. The Chosen One expected by the Hebrew people was to come in the form of a warrior-king, a leader who would destroy the enemies that threatened Israel's life.

So here is Jesus, who has just been proclaimed by John the Baptist to be the Messiah. Word is spreading, people are starting to believe that the prophecy has come true, and Jesus himself must have been touched by the emotional turmoil of this historical moment. Then comes the devil saying, "Go ahead and prove it. Prove that you are the Chosen One by doing mighty magic. Bolster your ego and win more believers by giving us evidence of who you are." Jesus, who may well have believed that he had a special calling from God, was given a chance to "prove" that calling to himself and to others with dramatic flair and finality.

Had Jesus seized that chance, he would have reminded us of some of the characters in Chuang Tzu's poem "Active Life": the strong man who needs weights to prove that he is strong, or the brave woman who needs an emergency to prove that she is brave. Chuang Tzu would have scoffed at a Messiah who needs a call for miracles to prove that he is a Messiah. Had Jesus made stone into bread simply to show the devil that he was the Chosen One, he would have been acting mechanically, caught in the cogs of cultural expectations, compelled by circumstances to act a role. By refusing to do so, he both demonstrates and extends his transcendence over the context of his action.

He does this in part simply by redefining "Chosen One" to suit his own sense of truth, without regard to cultural expectations. Jesus does not regard himself as accountable for his calling to any voice except God's, so in his refusal to "prove" anything to the devil he is actually proving that he *is* the Chosen One as he himself understands it. Of course, there is nothing simple about that; it is always a struggle to follow one's inner light.

When you refuse to meet the terms of an external demand, refuse to produce publicly verifiable results, you do not prove anything in the normal sense of that word. Instead, you leave yourself open to charges of evasion or cowardice, and you forfeit the external confirmation on which so many of us depend; you may become inwardly shaky about who you really are. Perhaps all of this was happening inside Jesus. If so, it makes this particular temptation all the more compelling in his life, as it is in ours.

But the testing that Jesus receives here is not only about his spiritual identity. It has also to do with the very practical matter of hunger. In light of the fact that Jesus had been fasting in the desert for an extended period of time "and at the end he was hungry," the devil seems to speak with a voice of reason, perhaps even compassion, when he says, ". . . Tell this stone to turn into a loaf." Henri Nouwen calls this the temptation to be *relevant,* and with that word he names something that many of us face from time to time—the temptation to "solve" some problem on a level that does not solve it at all, and may even make things worse.[5]

Jesus' real problem in the desert is not hunger—though it might look that way to an outside observer—so his real solution is not bread. When you fast for an extended period of time your body adjusts to the lack of food and does not become as ravenous as it does in the midst of a three-meal day. In fact, many people who fast report a depth of bodily well-being that eludes them when they are eating regularly. Furthermore, when the time comes to end a fast, you do so gradually, and at first only with liquids and soft foods; you do not devour a chunk of bread! When we rush to the aid of a fasting person, attempting to be "relevant" by insisting that he or she eat, we are likely not only to be irrelevant but to do harm as well.

True relevance requires a certain subtlety, which the very idea of relevance seems to exclude. What Jesus really needs in his desert fast is not food. In fact, he does not need anything external. Like the woodcarver, who fasted not merely from food but from praise and criticism, gain and success, Jesus' real need is for inward confirmation of his mission, a confirmation he is more likely to find in the emptiness of fasting than in the gratification of bodily needs. (This does not mean that spiritual fulfillment requires continual fasting. The Gospels suggest that Jesus, after his desert experience, sat and ate at more banquet tables than Herod and Nebuchadnezzar combined.)

Actions that seem relevant may turn out to be irrelevant in the extreme. Parents, for example, know that they do not necessarily solve a child's problem by giving in to the demand for a special toy. They must address the problem behind the problem, which may be the child's capacity for delayed gratification or for simple self-reliance. Teachers know that they do not necessarily solve a student's problem by answering the questions the student asks. The real question may be the student's ability to find answers for himself or herself, so the teacher who withholds answers may enlarge the student's capacity to learn. The temptation to be relevant is often the temptation to deal with only the external illusion of a problem and ignore its internal truth.

III. I WILL GIVE YOU POWER

In the second temptation, the devil takes Jesus up to a high place and gives him a vision of earthly glory and power. The devil says that the power and glory belong to him, but that he will give it all to Jesus if Jesus will worship him. But Jesus rejects this second bid with the scriptural injunction to serve God alone.

We have so many contemporary examples of this temptation to power that it is hard to know which to choose.[6] I remember hearing an interview with John Dean some years ago. He told of how, as a young lawyer in Washington, he was quickly seduced by the trappings of power when Nixon asked him to serve as the President's special counsel. There were Marine guards, flights in Air Force One, visits to the San Clemente compound, access to influence and fame. Dean, of course, became one of the key actors in the Watergate conspiracy that led to Nixon's resignation. Dean lived out his own version of Jesus' second temptation, as have many of us in less dramatic ways.

It is no accident that the devil led Jesus "to a height" in order to pose this temptation, no accident that John Dean was tempted by the power of the highest office in the land, no accident that Buber's angel "poured" his false blessings down to earth from the highest heavens. The power that tempts us is never power with or for others, but always power *over* something or someone. These images of height are more than literary gimmicks. They reveal two illusions we succumb to when we accept a power that promises to put us above it all.

The first illusion is that once we are above it all we need not be immersed in the suffering of those who are under our power. Whether we intend to use our power for good or for ill, it is comforting to imagine that it will keep us at a distance from distressing conditions. The second illusion is that a power that keeps us above it all is a power that will not corrupt us. No matter how suspect its source may be, such a power seems to remove us from that twisted world in which petty power ensnares mere mortals.

Jesus must have wrestled with these illusions as he stood there on the heights, above it all. Though the devil was the source of the power, Jesus must have toyed with the thought that this power would put him above and beyond its very source, allowing him to use it for godly, not devilish, purposes. And if Jesus intuited any of the suffering that was to come in his life, he must have been sorely tempted by a power that promised to allow him to do good without getting himself hurt.

But power is never a mere means, a neutral tool to be used this way or that, depending on our own moral strength. Every form of power contains its own moral trajectory, an ethical course and objective from which it is not likely to be deflected. The power that John Dean accepted from Richard Nixon had little flexibility, hedged about as it was by the limits of politics, of personal relations, of ego. In fact, the moral trajectory of Dean's power as special counsel to the President was so profoundly programmed that if Dean did not agree with its course, he could not redirect it but only reject it.

Power such as this has a life of its own. Once we have seized it, it seizes us, and wresting ourselves from its grip requires superhuman effort. If power over things seems at first like a tool, those who hold it may soon become tools trapped in power's own strong hands.

Reflections such as these may have helped Jesus reject the devil's seductive offer. But even more helpful might have been the simple but often unasked question, "Does this guy really have the thing he says he can give me?" The whole premise of this second temptation is the devil's claim that "all this power and the glory of these kingdoms . . . has been committed to me and I give it to anyone I choose." But is that true? The premise of Nixon's offer to Dean was surely an implicit claim that he could give a meaning and purpose to Dean's life that would exceed his wildest dreams. But were meaning and purpose ever Nixon's to give?

The answer is as obvious as the question. But we often fail to ask the question, which is testimony to the way that an offer of power can rob us of common sense. People cannot give away what they do not have, and yet a million exchanges are made every day in which people promise to do exactly that. The promises may not be explicit; they may arise as much from the greed of the recipient as from the guile of the promise-maker; but they are there and they are seductive, despite the fact that they are delusions, pure and simple.

Examples are endless. When people exchange money for a car, they are often buying more than transportation; they are buying a fantasy of freedom. When people pay money for an education, they expect more than knowledge, more than credits and degrees; they want status and dignity. When people buy into a health club they want more than exercise; they are often seeking friendship and a sense of community. It does not matter that the automakers or educators or fitness entrepreneurs cannot supply this "something more." It is implicit in the contract, it helps them sell the product, and many buyers never stop to ask whether the promise can be fulfilled.

When Jesus rejects the devil's offer of power and glory by quoting the scriptural injunction to worship and serve God alone, he is not being merely pious. Nor is he enunciating an ethical *ought*. He is stating a simple fact: Power and glory are not the devil's to give. They belong to God alone, and only through God can we share in them.

Were Jesus to worship the devil in this case, it would not be so much immoral as just plain foolish. The devil has power only as long as we allow him his pretenses. But once we strip those pretenses away, the devil becomes a pathetic figure, akin to those TV pitchmen who insist that you, too, can own three income-producing properties for only $29.95 plus postage. I wonder if the devil, stripped of his pretenses by Jesus, looked at all like Richard Nixon on the day he resigned, a man quite different from the one that John Dean saw on the day of his temptation, a hollow figure, a king who had no clothing?

IV. THROW YOURSELF DOWN

In this third temptation, the devil "led Jesus to Jerusalem and made him stand on the parapet of the Temple." Again the devil taunts Jesus with the words, "If you are the Chosen One . . . ," but this time the challenge is for Jesus to hurl himself off the parapet. After all, the devil reminds him, Scripture promises that your guardian angel will keep you from harm. But Jesus refuses, quoting the scriptural mandate not to put God to the test.

The fact that the devil "led" Jesus to Jerusalem and "made" him stand on the parapet of the Temple reminds us of how unresistant Jesus has been on one level of this story. He allowed himself to be led into the wilderness, then led to a height, and then led to the Temple—and each time, he went along without a fight or even any apparent reluctance. It may even be that he went with a certain eagerness to know what was coming next. In any event, he went, doubtless because he knew that if he refused this particular leading, it would simply come again under some other guise; he knew that sooner or later he would have to face the challenge and make a response. Why not now?

Perhaps the fact that Jesus does not resist being led into places of temptation allows him to save energy for the real resistance, for all the crucial "no's" that he must say to the devil. Resisting temptation does not mean refusing to go into places where one is tempted, does not mean evading the quandaries of one's life. We must go to those places because we have to, because they are necessary way stations on the journey, because the journey requires energy that should not be squandered on fighting the journey itself. The real work is to go where we are led, to see what is there, to respond out of our own truth.

Jesus' "no" to this third temptation may have been especially difficult because the devil, for the first time in their encounter, quotes Scripture to shore up his case. One can almost see the devil's mind at work. Having heard Jesus resist his demonic entreaties with scriptural references the first two times, the devil says to himself, "OK, two can play that game. . . . " But Jesus, undaunted, quotes the Scriptures right back.

Someone once said that all religious people are "selective fundamentalists," that we all emphasize whatever portions of Holy Writ serve our purposes at the moment. At very least, this dialogue between Jesus and the devil shows that right action cannot come simply from The Book, or from any book. The truth behind right action is not propositional but personal. It must come not from outside the person but from within.

The devil stands outside the words he quotes; he uses them merely to manipulate Jesus. But Jesus stands inside his words; he believes them, or they would not give him power. Furthermore, the words Jesus quotes are more fundamental, in the true sense, than those the devil chooses. While the devil engages in airy speculation about angelic assistance, Jesus invokes a bedrock truth about our relation to God: "You must not put the Lord your God to the test."

Again, I think we misread these words if we understand them as an *ought,* an ethical commandment. They are simply factual. We have no way to test God even if we wanted to, no way (in this case) to alter the laws that apply to physical beings in a material universe. I do not think it would be morally wrong to test God by jumping off a high building to see if God would save you. It would simply be stupid. Such a jump would be the consequence not of moral depravity but of being out of touch with certain basic realities. Jesus resists the devil not with superior ethics or biblical scholarship but with common sense, a sense of what is real.

(There are, of course, crucial differences between Jesus wisely refusing to test the law of gravity in this story and the angel boldly trying to break the law of suffering in Buber's tale. Jesus is invited by the devil to take this act, but it is God who evokes and empowers the angel's act. Jesus would act for himself alone; the angel acts partly on behalf of others. The law of gravity is physical and cannot be broken, only modified by other physical laws; the law of suffering is of the heart and can be mitigated by true compassion.)

Henri Nouwen calls this third temptation the temptation to be *spectacular,* and it may be the most difficult of the three to resist.[7] If you and I were to become known as relevant and powerful people, we would find ourselves burdened by the responsibilities that come with the image. If you make bread you have to deal with the hungry, and if you become king you have the headaches that come with governing. But no such burdens accompany a reputation for being spectacular. This is, perhaps, the temptation to be charismatic, to inspire the sort of awe in people that leaves your ego continually inflated but that lacks the obligations that might pull you back to earth. A person who could jump unharmed off the parapet of the Temple would at least get invited to a lot of parties, and might even have access to influence and wealth if he or she played it right.

The temptation to perform an act that has no rationale except to make yourself known is an insidious one in our media age—an age when, as Andy Warhol has said too often, everyone can expect to be famous for fifteen minutes. But the media only amplify the anguish of mass society, the anguish of people who feel utterly insignificant and unknown. Every day we witness the pain of people who need to cry out, "Look! I'm here! I have power! I count!" That cry comes in many forms, some of them pathological—the loner who guns down innocents on a school playground to make a mark, the person who attempts suicide to get attention, people who live self-destructive lifestyles to make themselves known. The temptation to be spectacular may seem laughable in the abstract, but some of its manifestations are the stuff of modern tragedy.

V. THE TEMPTATION TO BE INADEQUATE

Many people are seduced from time to time by the temptations to be relevant, powerful, or spectacular, and a few people have to wrestle with them regularly. But perhaps the more common temptation for most of us is to feel that we have little or no chance to be any of these things, even if we wanted to. Many of us awake each day with so little self-confidence that the thought of being offered a chance at power and glory seems absurd. The temptations Jesus faced are those of the strong ego. But the temptation that afflicts many of us is that of the weak ego—the temptation to think of ourselves as irrelevant, powerless, and utterly mundane, as people in whom Satan would never have the slightest interest.

On the surface, the temptations of the strong ego and the weak ego seem quite contrary to one another. But paradoxically, their origins and outcomes are the same. Both destroy our capacity for right action because both proceed from the same mistaken premise: the assumption that effective action requires us to be relevant, powerful, and spectacular, that only by being so can we have a real impact on the world.

People with strong egos, who think they can have what the devil is selling, are tempted to do business with him so that they can be "effective." If they make a deal, they end up doing damage to themselves and the world in ways that we have already explored. But people with weak egos, who think that the devil would pass them by without a glance or nod, are tempted to believe that they have no way of acting effectively. They, too, end up doing damage to themselves and to the world. They damage themselves with feelings of inadequacy that diminish their birthright gifts; they damage the world by withdrawing from action and leaving the world's fate to the aggressive few. No matter which set of temptations one succumbs to, both the self and the world are damaged, for both sets are rooted in the destructive illusion that we need what the devil is peddling if we are to lead active lives of any consequence or worth.

Jesus' ability to see through this illusion is clearly at the core of his resistance to the devil. He knows that right action does not require us to be relevant, powerful, or spectacular. Right action requires only that we respond faithfully to our own inner truth and to the truth around us. It requires not that we aim at any particular outcome, for ourselves or for others, but that we act on truth as we know it, with truth as our only end. Right action is no more or less than the action it is right to take, taken without anxiety about results. If an action is rightly taken, taken with integrity, its outcomes will achieve whatever is possible—which is the best that anyone can do.

The ultimate paradox of right action, not always but often, is that its outcomes may well be relevant, powerful, and spectacular. Nowhere is that paradox better illustrated than in the stories of Jesus' own active life. As soon as Jesus dispensed with the devil, resisting the three temptations with sweat and blood, he embarked on a life of action that was relevant, powerful, and spectacular in the extreme. His healings were certainly spectacular, to say nothing of his Resurrection. He clearly exercised power; he changed the course of history. And he was relevant as well. In fact, one of the most famous stories about him, the miracle of the loaves and fishes (which will be the focus of the next chapter), shows him taking the very action that he refused to take in the desert—making bread, apparently by magic. What is going on in this strange reversal?

One clue is found in the three lines at the end of the temptations tale:

Having exhausted all these ways of tempting him, the devil left him, to return at the appointed time. Jesus, with the power of the Spirit in him, returned to Galilee; and his reputation spread throughout the countryside. He taught in their synagogues and everyone praised him.

Although these lines seem to be saying three different things, they are, in good storytelling fashion, making the same point in three different ways: The temptations have not gone away, despite what Jesus has been through. They will arise over and over in Jesus' active life—and in our own. Temptation is not a one-time thing, finally resolved, any more than revelation or being "born again" is once and for all. These things happen again and again (at least, they do if we are alive), for they are the dynamics of the life process itself.

The first line in the passage above explicitly makes this point when it says that the devil will return to Jesus at the "appointed time." Some people take that to foretell the crucifixion, when Jesus was tempted to believe that he had been abandoned by God, tempted perhaps to run away from his destiny. But I think that the reference is much broader than that, that the "appointed time" comes up continually in the course of the active life, as the second and third lines of the passage suggest.

The second line says that Jesus returned to Galilee "with the power of the Spirit in him" (the same Spirit, of course, that led him into his desert encounter with the devil) and that "his reputation spread throughout the countryside." The word *reputation* should alert us to the fact that Jesus' temptations are not over. Anyone who acts in the power of the Spirit is going to gain a reputation as a compelling person. When that happens, temptation grows—the temptation to believe one's press clippings, to believe that one's reputation is a true mirror of one's soul, to give other people only what they want so that one's reputation can grow larger, to act more and more for the sake of reputation and less and less in the light of right action.

It seems clear that Jesus had to wrestle with this temptation throughout his active life. For example, we have the story of Jesus gathering his disciples and asking them, "Who do the people say that I am?" (Luke 9:18–26, RSV). It is not clear why he asks the question, but obviously he feels a need to wrestle with the issue of his public reputation. When the disciples reply that the people say he is Elijah, or John the Baptist, or one of the prophets, Jesus tries to penetrate these public images by asking, "But who do *you* say that I am?" He is trying to deflect his public reputation by asking his intimates to name his truth themselves. When Peter answers, "You are the Christ," the story says that Jesus "charged them to tell no one about him." Surely, this exchange shows how Jesus had to keep struggling with the temptations posed by his growing reputation.

The last line of the temptations story says all of this again, in slightly different words: ". . . Everyone praised him." Once one has overcome the temptation to be relevant, powerful, and spectacular—or the temptation to believe that one cannot act for lack of these qualities—one may suddenly become quite winsome and subject to praise. Such a person can easily appear to the public to be everything he or she has resisted being, and life can become very confusing. Having renounced any effort to gain praise, because praise is not a valid goal, one suddenly finds oneself being praised for the renunciation! For such people the dynamic of temptation seems never to end.

I have known people caught in this dynamic; in fact, in our age of mass media, it is not uncommon. I know a man who has spoken so powerfully of the human need for solitude that he has touched many people, only to find his followers clamoring so incessantly for his presence that solitude is about the last thing he can have. There are two problems at work here. One is the public's tendency to project onto this man a quality that they want to possess but are unable to find in themselves, so they burden their hero with the impossible task of living out a part of their lives for them. The other problem is that their hero, like most of us, may find the hero role attractive, may seek to keep those projections coming, may even be willing to give up the solitary life that he finds so valuable for the sake of praise and fame—as I might, if given the chance.

About the first problem, there is little that my friend can do. But the second problem is more malleable, and for some people in the active life, solving it is very nearly a matter of life and death. One can resist the destructive projections that people often make, by being relentlessly honest about one's own reality, as Jesus is throughout the tale of the temptations. One can fend off the illusions of others by staying rooted in one's own truth.

A moving example of this sort of honesty is found in the life of the German poet, Rainer Maria Rilke. A young poet asked the master for guidance, and the older man responded generously in letter after letter of encouragement, criticism, and wisdom. But as their correspondence came to an end, Rilke must have sensed that the young man was lionizing him, letting Rilke's hard-won wisdom substitute for the work that the young poet needed to do to find wisdom of his own. So in one of his final letters, Rilke wrote

And if there is one more thing that I must say to you, it is this: Don't think that the person who is trying to comfort you now lives untroubled among the simple and quiet words that sometimes give you pleasure. His life has much trouble and sadness, and remains far behind yours. If it were otherwise, he would never have been able to find those words.[8]

Rilke is trying to resist illusion with his own truth. But even as we read that winsome passage, we can sense temptation's eternal return. Rilke's honesty about his own limitations makes him even more attractive, even more a candidate for lionization. Whether those words turned the young poet to his own inner work, I do not know. But if Rilke understood his own words, they must have helped Rilke guard his spirit against the same temptations that the devil posed to Jesus.

Whether we lust after them or regard them as out of reach, those three devilish temptations are at once the most common norms for action and the most misleading guides to a life of right action. Right action demands that we find a deeper and truer source of energy and guidance than relevance, power, and spectacle can provide. Some images of that deeper source will emerge as we explore one more Jesus tale, this one from the midst of his life of public caring.

7. "Loaves and Fishes": Acts of Scarcity or Abundance

I. THE FEEDING OF THE FIVE THOUSAND

A good teacher, it is said, does not give all the answers, but leaves his or her students with lots of questions. If that is true, then the story of Jesus feeding five thousand people with five loaves of bread and two fish is a very good teacher indeed. I do not know any story purporting to be historical that leaves us with as many questions as this one—except, of course, for many of the other stories about Jesus' active life. About such tales the words of Black Elk, the Native American shaman, are worth pondering: "Whether it happened so or not I do not know; but if you think about it you can see that it is true."[1]

"The Miracle of the Loaves and Fishes"

The apostles returned to Jesus, and told him all that they had done and taught. And he said to them, "Come away by yourselves to a lonely place, and rest a while." For many were coming and going, and they had no leisure even to eat. And they went away in the boat to a lonely place by themselves. Now many saw them going, and knew them, and they ran there on foot from all the towns, and got there ahead of them. As he landed he saw a great throng, and he had compassion on them, because they were like sheep without a shepherd; and he began to teach them many things. And when it grew late, his disciples came to him and said, "This is a lonely place, and the hour is now late; send them away, to go into the country and villages round about and buy themselves something to eat." But he answered them, "You give them something to eat." And they said to him, "Shall we go and buy two hundred denarii worth of bread, and give it to them to eat?" And he said to them, "How many loaves have you? Go and see." And when they had found out, they said, "Five, and two fish." Then he commanded them all to sit down by companies upon the green grass. So they sat down in groups, by hundreds and by fifties. And taking the five loaves and the two fish he looked up to heaven, and blessed, and broke the loaves, and gave them to the disciples to set before the people; and he divided the two fish among them all. And they all ate and were satisfied. And they took up twelve baskets full of the broken pieces and of the fish. And those who ate the loaves were five thousand people. (Mark 6:30–44, RSV).*

This story is laced with the paradoxical interplay of contemplation and action. It begins with the disciples returning to Jesus to tell him how busy they have been. Seeing that they are weary with work, Jesus urges them to retreat to "a lonely place" where they might "rest a while." So off they go, seeking only a quiet interlude in their active lives. But their movement draws attention, and by the time their boat arrives, this lonely place is packed with people who had run ahead to see what Jesus and his disciples might be up to now. When Jesus and his disciples seek contemplation, they ironically evoke more action.

The story tells us that contemplation and action cannot be separated the way that we separate work and vacation. Action will always set up the need for contemplation. But true contemplation is never a mere retreat. Instead, it draws us deeper into right action by getting us more deeply in touch with the gifts that we have to give, with our need to give them, with the people and problems that need us. As the story shows, Jesus and his disciples cannot take a vacation from the reality of their lives, from the consequences of that reality for the people around them. The deeper they go into contemplation, the more clearly their true work emerges, the more others call for

---

* Text slightly altered for the sake of inclusive language.

it, and the more the disciples feel the claim of that work on their lives.

But the contemplative idyll that Jesus and his disciples sought was thwarted not only by the presence of the clamoring crowd, but by Jesus himself, the one who had urged this outing in the first place. He "had compassion" on the throng "because they were like sheep without a shepherd," and he apparently could not keep himself from teaching them until "it grew late." Jesus might have driven the crowd away, insisting that he and his disciples needed rest, or he might have escaped further into the wilderness. But no, he had to see the crowd's need and respond to it—which must have wearied the disciples even more.

In his response to the crowd, is Jesus acting like the people in Chuang Tzu's satire "Active Life," people who need so badly to be needed that their actions are no more than knee-jerk reactions to external stimuli? Those people are "prisoners in the world of objects," and their actions are dictated by the turnings of interlocking cogs. Is Jesus like that, a teacher who would pine away if he did not have someone to teach, an activist who leaps into action at the slightest excuse?

I do not think so, partly on the evidence of this story and partly in light of other stories about his teaching. There were times when Jesus refused to teach or, when he was pressed to do so, offered teachings so opaque that he might as well have refused. In fact, there are enough stories about Jesus fleeing the clamoring crowd that he can hardly be accused of behaving like a firehorse at the clanging of any bell. If he proved anything with the devil in the desert, he proved that he was perfectly capable of resisting false action.

In this story, Jesus' teaching begins with his feeling of compassion for the throng, and compassion is a quality that makes action responsive rather than reflexive. Compassionate *feeling with* other people is precisely what the automatons in Chuang Tzu's satire cannot do. Chuang Tzu's actors all believe that they possess some special attribute that sets them

apart from others—a wisdom or strength or skill that no one
else has. Because they regard themselves as superior, they are
incapable of acting except for the sake of self-interest and self-
image. Like Buber's angel, they have none of the brokenness,
none of the humility, that make it possible to act for, and
with, other people.

Compassionate action of the sort that Jesus takes in this story
begins with a deep identity between the actor and the others.
Jesus can see that the crowd is "like sheep without a shepherd"
because he knows intimately their feelings of loneliness, aban-
donment, fear. Though we do not know the content of his
teaching in this story, we know from many other stories that
Jesus teaches from his own life, including his experience in the
desert; he teaches the hard-won insights of a life lived at the
depths. He does not teach to prove himself, nor does he teach
what the crowd wants to hear. He teaches to feed the people's
authentic hungers, offering a meal of wisdom that is the essential context for the meal of fish and bread soon to come.

Hunger and food, of both the literal and metaphorical sorts,
are the dominant images in this story. I want to translate these
images into the generic terms of scarcity and abundance. The
crowd that seeks a teacher does so because it finds truth
scarce; Jesus teaches to reveal truth's abundance. The disciples, asked to feed the crowd, are sure that food is scarce; Jesus
performs a "miracle" to reveal how abundant food is even
when there is none in sight. In this story, as throughout his
active life, Jesus wanted to help people penetrate the illusion
of scarcity and act out of the reality of abundance.

II. THE SCARCITY ASSUMPTION

The quality of our active lives depends heavily on whether
we assume a world of scarcity or a world of abundance. Do
we inhabit a universe where the basic things that people
need—from food and shelter to a sense of competence and of
being loved—are ample in nature? Or is this a universe where
such goods are in short supply, available only to those who

have the power to beat everyone else to the store? The nature of our action will be heavily conditioned by the way we answer those bedrock questions. In a universe of scarcity, only people who know the arts of competing, even of making war, will be able to survive. But in a universe of abundance, acts of generosity and community become not only possible but fruitful as well.

Given the sort of action that dominates our world, it is apparent that many of us, and our institutions, have chosen the scarcity assumption. How else can you explain such practices as grading on the curve, an educational device that treats *A*'s and *B*'s as if they were diamonds, while treating *C*'s and *D*'s as if we had warehouses full of them? How else can you explain the fact that competition (a way of allocating scarcity), rather than cooperation (a way of sharing abundance), is widely regarded as the only way to conduct our affairs, to make things happen? How else can you explain the fact that our country so fearfully clings to its habit of overconsuming the world's resources, as if letting other people have a fair share would mean national suicide? At every level of our lives the assumption of scarcity, not abundance, threatens to deform our attitudes and our actions.

Tragically, every time we act on the scarcity assumption, we help create a world in which scarcity becomes a cruel reality. When we Americans, who comprise some six percent of the world's population, consume over a third of the world's resources, we create real scarcity for others. When employers insist on pitting people against each other for raises and promotions, rather than rewarding people for corporate creativity, workplaces become snake pits in which people will do nearly anything to survive. When teachers grade on the curve, education becomes a process of progressive discouragement for too many students, and only a small elite end up believing they have ability.

The scarcity assumption pervades our institutional life by putting power into the hands of a few, and keeping it there. Hierarchies are always rooted in the belief that power itself is, or ought to be, a scarce commodity, rooted in the belief that few people are qualified to hold power, or that few should be allowed to hold it, lest the threatening abundance of power known as "democracy" come to pass. From the teacher who grades on the curve to the administrator who rules by fiat, the control of the few over the many is rationalized by the scarcity assumption.

It is sobering to realize that this assumption can be found not only in our institutional politics but in the depths of our personal lives. Therapists are kept in business partly by the common fear that such personal goods as love, affirmation, and esteem are in very short supply. If we understood that there is an infinite supply of love for every person, more than enough to go around, we would not compete for affection with those around us or fall into despair when we feel that we are not getting our share. A primary task for every healer is to help people understand that love is not distributed on the curve but is abundant in the very nature of things.

In the story of the loaves and fishes, Jesus makes a dramatic attempt to break people of the scarcity habit by revealing the reality of abundance. The drama begins when the disciples come to Jesus, saying that the hour is late, that Jesus should disperse the crowd to nearby villages to buy dinner for themselves. Two things are happening here, two things that reflect and reinforce the assumption of scarcity.

The first is the disciples' insistence that the people be told to buy their evening meal. The disciples obviously believe that food is scarce, and when something is scarce we are conditioned to think that it must be distributed competitively. The most efficient way to do that is through the impersonal intermediary called money.

The cash-exchange mechanism makes it so much easier for us to ignore the gross inequities in the distribution of food and shelter around our world. If governments were to line people up each month, giving a few of them truckloads of food while giving the majority barely enough to survive, the inequity would be so visible, so maddening, that revolution might ensue. Instead, we arrange for a few private people to receive truckloads of money, while the majority receive much less. When we exchange our dollars for whatever food they will buy, the transaction is so veiled that only the hungry and powerless see what is going on. The impersonal medium of money has so distanced us from injustice that there is little pressure for change. Jesus' disciples, convinced that scarcity reigns, want people to buy their own dinners so that the cash economy can obscure the "fact" that there is too little food to go around.

The second thing happening as this drama begins is intimately related to the first. Not only do the disciples want people to buy their own dinners; they also want to disperse them, to "send them away, to go into the country and villages round about. . . . " That is, the disciples want people to compete separately and individually for scarce food, rather than join together in a community that has the potential for sharing, for generating abundance in the midst of scarcity. I wonder if this is the first recorded example of Reaganomics?

There is a powerful correlation between the assumption of scarcity and the decline of community, a correlation that runs both ways. If we allow the scarcity assumption to dominate our thinking, we will act in individualistic, competitive ways that destroy community. If we destroy community, where creating and sharing with others generates abundance, the scarcity assumption will become more valid.

When we are in community, many things that we think we must buy in the marketplace suddenly become available free of charge. For example, some of the personal attention and care that many people now purchase from therapists may be available from members of a community organized to offer mutual aid. Expensive equipment that must be owned by every family unit in our fragmented society can be shared by numbers of people in a community. Simple maintenance and repair services that we normally purchase are often offered at little or no cost in a community of diverse skills. Entertainment, which we buy in the form of professional events or electronic equipment, is available without charge in a community where human intrigue, drama, and comedy are the stuff of everyday life. Community and abundance go hand in hand; the two words are nearly synonymous.

It is fascinating to see how Jesus responds to the disciples when they urge him to disperse the five thousand to buy their own dinners. Simply, but pointedly, he tells them, "You give them something to eat." With the word "you," Jesus turns the tables on his disciples. Instead of allowing them to palm the problem of dinner off onto the crowd, he puts the problem back into the disciples' own hands. With the word "give," Jesus turns the tables once again. Instead of allowing the disciples to deal with the dinner problem impersonally, through cash exchange, Jesus names it as a problem to be solved through an act of generosity. Implicit in his words is the understanding that both community and abundance can be generated when we turn from buying to giving, from making people compete to offering of ourselves.

But the disciples, like some of us, are slow learners. No sooner has Jesus said, "You give them something to eat" than the disciples ask him, "Shall we go and buy two hundred denarii worth of bread, and give it to them to eat?" Though they may have accepted their own responsibility to feed the people, they persist in thinking that the best way to exercise that responsibility is through cash exchange. So Jesus takes one more step toward the disciples' enlightenment, and ours, by responding with a question and a command: "How many loaves have you? Go and see."

Here is a crucial turning point in our transition from assuming scarcity to seeing the potentials of abundance. It consists in the simple but rare act of looking at what we already have, at the gifts and resources that are immediately available to us. Our activism sometimes breeds the arrogant belief that nothing exists except as we make it, buy it, sell it, or get a grant for it. The truth is, of course, that we could not make anything, let alone buy or sell it, if nothing existed in the first place; our making is always a mixing of our ideas and energies with the abundant gifts of nature. So the first step in any action that assumes abundance and wants to amplify it is to perceive, and receive, those resources already present to us in the abundance of life itself.

III. THE TRUE MIRACLE

"How many loaves have you? Go and see." The disciples follow Jesus' instructions, but the inventory they bring back to Jesus is hardly reassuring. The five loaves and two fish seem like textbook examples of scarcity when the problem is to feed five thousand hungry people. But Jesus does not hesitate. He gathers the crowd into small groups and seats them on the grass. He takes the loaves and fish and blesses them; he breaks them into pieces and gives them to the disciples to "set before the people." When all the people have eaten and are satisfied, twelve baskets full of leftovers remain.

What is going on here, and what can it possibly tell us about action and abundance in the real world? As the story reaches its climax it seems more and more unreal, the tale of a magician who can suspend the laws of nature and do things that have never been done before or since. That interpretation, one that focuses on a supernatural Jesus, does not make the story useful to ordinary activists, much as we would like to be miracle workers too. In fact, that interpretation can easily lead us to shirk our human responsibility for others. It could allow us to say about the feeding of the five thousand, as the people around the woodcarver said of the bell stand, "It must be the work of spirits."

An alternative interpretation begins with the reminder that the Jesus who makes bread multiply here is the same Jesus who refused to make bread by magic when challenged to do so by the devil. If the feeding of the five thousand were no more than a magic act, I think we could hear the devil off in the distance chuckling, "I won!" It seems unlikely that Jesus would sacrifice his integrity by doing tricks here on the lakeshore when he fought so hard to preserve his integrity against the devil's taunts in the desert.

What Jesus does instead of magic is to act on the assumption of abundance. First, he divides the crowd into "companies" of hundreds and fifties and commands them all "to sit down . . . upon the green grass." His miracle begins with the simple act of gathering the faceless crowd of five thousand into smaller, face-to-face communities. This is the stock-in-trade of every good community organizer, this clustering of people into more intimate settings where everyday miracles have a chance to happen.

We can imagine what happens among the people as Jesus replaces the dulling anonymity of the crowd with the energy and personalism of human-scale groups. Friends and neighbors spot each other. People greet and embrace, full of the joy of recognition and the excitement of the event. Animated words are exchanged about this phenomenon called Jesus and about the strange events surrounding his life. On many levels and in many ways this collection of isolated individuals is re-collected into the organic, interactive reality of life together.

I said earlier that community is the context in which abundance can replace scarcity. Even more important, the very experience of community is itself an experience of abundance. In the faceless crowd we experience scarcity—a scarcity of contact, of concern, of affirmation, of love. But as the crowd is replaced by community, an invisible sense of abundance arises long before the community produces any visible goods or services. True abundance resides in the simple experience of people being present to one another and for one another. Only in such a context of interpersonal abundance could the material abundance of food aplenty even begin to arise.

I do not demand a naturalistic explanation for the "miracle" in this story; I am content to let the story be story and to learn from it on that level. But since this story purports to be rooted in historical events, it is intriguing to speculate on what may have happened.

According to the text, Jesus asks the disciples, "How many loaves have you?" It is unclear whether the "you" refers to the disciples themselves, or to the entire crowd, but I would guess the former; a moment earlier Jesus has told the disciples, "*You* give them something to eat." He seems to be trying to get the disciples to understand that they have a gift to give the crowd that does not depend on stockpiles of food or on commercial transactions.

Then the text says that Jesus blessed and broke the five loaves and two fish and had the disciples set them before the people. It does not say that the loaves and fish had magically multiplied by the time they left Jesus' hands. What may have happened instead is that Jesus and the disciples simply modeled the act of sharing for the crowd by giving thanks for what little they had and then offering it to any who wanted to eat.

As this happened, perhaps the people gathered in the small groups realized that they, too, had food they could share with one another. Perhaps they found themselves moved to emulate the generosity of Jesus and the disciples rather than hoard their scarce resources. In fact, it might have been hard to do otherwise, sitting there on the grass in a circle of family and friends and neighbors, watching this beleaguered little band of Jesus' followers giving away their own meager rations. Suddenly, through a community ignited by an example of generosity, scarcity turns into abundance. It happens not by magic but by the live encounter of people who have been helped to *re-member* each other and themselves, who have been brought back to what Chuang Tzu calls their "right minds" by an action in which abundance is both assumed and generated.

The story does not claim that everyone walked away from the dinner with a full belly. It simply says, "And they all ate and were satisfied." Here, it seems to me, is a true miracle: that everyone in a group of two or more, let alone five thousand, should end up satisfied. The culture of scarcity thrives on dissatisfaction, and breeds it as well. Our refusal to believe that we have enough is one cause of the competition that has resulted in such an inequitable distribution of resources at home and around the world. But a culture of abundance both arises from and creates a sense of satisfaction. In such a culture, enough is enough, and the very fact that people are willing to share scarcity in community produces a satisfaction that leads to more sharing, more abundance.

The people around Jesus must have been satisfied on many levels. They had experienced Jesus' compassion for them, his willingness to meet them at their point of need rather than running from them or driving them away. They had heard his teaching, a teaching that had come from deep within his own heart and had reached deep into theirs hearts. They had experienced both the excitement of being in a crowd of seekers and the fulfillment of being clustered into small communities that allowed for mutual caring. They had shared a meal with one another, a meal of abundance that had arisen from apparent scarcity. These people must have sensed that they were participants in a wonderful event, one in which a new reality was being revealed, a reality far removed from the conventional wisdom but as close at hand as the human heart. No wonder, then, that "all . . . were satisfied."

When we see the many ways in which the five thousand were fed, we can turn with fresh understanding to the words with which Jesus rebuffs the devil in the first temptation: "People do not live on bread alone." He does not mean that we should not feed hungry people. He is stating the simple truth that human beings are such a complex interaction of body and spirit that they can never be fully satisfied in body alone. Surely the five thousand were satisfied because Jesus had addressed them as whole persons, honored them at every level of authentic human need. Whenever that happens, scarcity is turned into abundance, and even a few scraps of fish and bread can seem like a banquet spread before us.

I sometimes ask people if they have ever experienced anything as "miraculous" as the feeding of the five thousand. Many say they have, for miracles of this sort are well within the realm of everyday life. I have known several myself, one of which so closely parallels the miracle of the loaves and fishes that, ever since it happened, the Gospel story has seemed eminently plausible to me.

For ten years I lived in an intentional community that was often graced by residents from abroad. One of them was a highly placed official in the government of the People's Republic of China, a member of the Communist party, and a man whose inner light was as strong and steady as any I have every known.

One day this man offered to cook a Chinese dinner for eight of us, and we quickly accepted. I drove him to the grocery store and, though I already had twenty dollars in my wallet, I stopped at the bank on the way. Unconsciously, I assumed that we would need to purchase the cartload of groceries that is customary, say, for a middle-class American Thanksgiving. Like the disciples, I was certain that this feeding would require a good deal of cash.

Once inside the store, my Chinese friend purchased only enough vegetables, eggs, rice, and a few other items to fill a small bag. We paid ten dollars or so and headed home.

He gathered us in the kitchen and showed us how to help prepare the meal. We found spices, brought out pots and pans, made sauces, separated eggs, and chopped those vegetables so fine that I thought they would disappear. Instead, they multiplied, and so did our joy. We spent the better part of the afternoon in that kitchen, talking and laughing and learning.

The actual cooking took hardly any time. Six or eight dishes were prepared and set on the table before an astonished group. From that small bag of groceries had emerged a dinner large enough to satisfy all of us—a satisfaction that was laced with the joy that we took in our Chinese friend, the wonder of sharing in his rich and ancient culture (which had been closed to us for so many years), the delight of each other's company, and the sense that we had somehow stepped closer to world peace. The alchemy of love had turned scarcity into abundance, and since that day I have had no trouble believing that the feeding of the five thousand happened exactly as Mark tells the tale.

IV. LEADERSHIP FOR COMMUNITY

The miracle of the loaves and fishes begins with Jesus and his disciples trying to take a contemplative break from their work ("Come away by yourselves to a lonely place, and rest a while"), only to be thwarted by a crowd that demands their attention. But Jesus does not cling to the notion that contemplation can happen only when we are in silence and in solitude. Instead, he turns this entire event into an occasion for contemplation, and in doing so he reveals again the paradox of contemplation and action.

In an earlier chapter, I defined contemplation as any way that we unmask illusion and reveal reality. In this story the actions of Jesus give thousands of people a chance to penetrate the illusion of scarcity and touch the reality of abundance. But this contemplative moment is hardly quiet and withdrawn; it is a public event, replete with energy and movement. We have witnessed such events in our own time, under the leadership of Gandhi, Martin Luther King, Jr., and Dorothy Day—people gifted at public actions that create contemplative opportunities for those with eyes to see and ears to hear. If we could better understand the nature of such actions, we might be able to act accordingly in smaller but still significant ways.

To understand Jesus' capacity to draw a crowd into public contemplation, we must return to a brief but crucial moment in the story, the moment when Jesus takes the five loaves and two fish, and looks up to heaven, and blesses them. In that heavenward gaze and blessing, Jesus reveals at least two convictions that empower his action. First, he is giving his thanks for the food, acknowledging that he and the others depend on gifts beyond their making, acknowledging that gifts have in fact been given. Second, he is expressing his trust that there is a power other than his own at work in the situation, a power that frees him from the impossible burden of total responsibility for what happens, and thus frees him to act responsively.

There is a fine line here, this line involving gratitude for gifts and dependence on a power other than our own. On one side of the line stands Jesus, whose gratitude and dependence not only empower him to act but bring urgency to his action. On the other side of the line stand some of us, who use the idea of God's gifts to excuse ourselves from the responsibility of acting. "Let God do it," or "God will take care of things," are the baldest formulations of this spiritual evasion, but it can take more subtle and sophisticated forms as well. In fact, this religious rationalization for not acting is sometimes raised to theological status.

I know that God acts. But I believe that God can only act incarnationally through the various forms of embodiment that God takes on earth, including our own human form. There is no way for God to act if we, and other created beings, are unwilling or unable to give substance to God's yearnings, God's energies, God's will. We must discern the gifts God gives us, accept them, employ them, pass them along. Without our active cooperation, God's abundance remains in the realm of potential, always there, always available, but forever untapped. To put it into Christian terms, we are called to incarnate the Christ-life.

Unfortunately, one influential interpretation of the incarnation holds Jesus to be the one-and-only embodiment of the Christ-life in all of space and time. At worst, this has led to the encapsulated Jesus, a holy icon imprisoned in a glass case, unavailable for relationship except as a distant object of adoration. At best, this understanding of Jesus has led to a "great man" theory of history (and this theory is always about "men"). Here, Jesus remains unique, but a few men—like Abraham Lincoln or Pope John XXIII—are regarded as having had some Christ-like qualities, able to act alone, as Jesus did, to make things happen. At best, and at worst, the theology that makes Jesus a one-and-only incarnation of the Christ tends to excuse the rest of us from responding to human hungers with everyday actions that incarnate God's abundance.

I believe that every human being is an incarnation of the holy, that we all have the potential to live out that holiness. But a holy life is not merely a life of individual greatness. It is a life that evokes the power inherent in the community that we have with each other and with God, the power of corporate abundance that lies behind the illusion of scarcity.

In the feeding of the five thousand, Jesus (unlike Buber's angel) did not act alone—and that is the key to his "miracle." He acted in concert with others and evoked the abundance of community. Ultimately, the "body of Christ," so central to incarnational theology, is not the physical body of Jesus but the corporate body of those who gather around the Spirit, wherever it is found.

But even as we act to evoke community, we must remember that community itself is a gift to be received, not a goal to be achieved. We have a strong tendency to make community one more project among many, to struggle and strain to come into relationship with one another, only to find that the stress of these very efforts exhausts us and drives us apart. Still, time after time we try to "make" community happen in the same effortful and self-defeating ways. Why? Because as long as we are the makers, we remain in control; and as long as we are in control, we will not be vulnerable to the risks of true community.

True community, like all gifts, involves true risks. Community may or may not happen, may or may not be received, may or may not have consequences we like. As we read the story of the loaves and fishes today, two thousand years removed, we might easily imagine that Jesus knew exactly what the outcome of his action would be—just as a magician knows the outcome of every trick he performs. But miracles are not magic, and Jesus did not act with guarantees attached any more than we do. When Jesus attempted to evoke the power of community, to reveal the reality of abundance beneath the illusion of scarcity, his attempt might well have backfired. He could have found himself in the midst of a hungry and angry crowd that refused to let go of the scarcity illusion, that refused to take responsibility for its own well-being.

Worse still, when we cut through the scarcity illusion and trigger a communal act of abundance, we take the considerable risk of angering the powers-that-be. Political power often depends on perpetuating the illusion of scarcity, and anyone who reveals the communal potential for abundance may feel the wrath of those in high places. After all, Jesus was executed not because he failed to reveal abundance but because he managed to reveal it so compellingly. The same can be said of Gandhi and Martin Luther King, Jr., and many other leaders who empowered a community to act.

But despite all these risks, Jesus does not hesitate to exercise his power—the power of his radical openness to the gift of community, his openness to both its problems and its potentials. In the simple gesture of looking toward heaven and offering thanks, Jesus throws himself upon mercy—the mercy of God, yes, but also the mercy of the crowd. He has no assurances; he might be throwing himself to the wolves. But when he makes himself so vulnerable with his gesture of gratitude and dependence, he evokes a similar vulnerability within the people, giving them a chance to acknowledge and act upon the abundance each of them possesses. People do not always respond accordingly, but in this case they do, and the reality of corporate abundance is revealed.

If this particular train of grace had not been set in motion, Jesus could have done nothing to make community happen.

Jesus exercises the only kind of leadership that can evoke authentic community—a leadership that risks failure (and even crucifixion) by making space for other people to act. When a leader takes up all the space and preempts all the action, he or she may make something happen, but that something is not community. Nor is it abundance, because the leader is only one person and one person's resources invariably run out. But when a leader is willing to trust the abundance that people have and can generate together, willing to take the risk of inviting people to share from that abundance, then and only then may true community emerge.[2]

When we approach community as a project that can succeed if only we have the right technique, the right setting, the right goals, the right people, we are on the wrong track. Community and its abundance are always there, free gifts of grace that sustain our lives. The question is whether we will be able to perceive those gifts and receive them. That is likely to happen only when someone performs a vulnerable public act, assuming abundance but aware that others may cling to the illusion of scarcity. That is the kind of risky action that makes Jesus' story, and ours, worth the telling.

8. "Threatened with Resurrection": Acts of Death or New Life

I. THE HORIZONS OF ACTION

Every life is lived toward a horizon, a distant vision of what lies ahead. The quality of our action depends heavily on whether that horizon is dark with death or full of light and life. When we imagine ourselves moving toward the finality of death, our action may become deformed. We may become paralyzed, unable to act freely. We may become driven by fear, obsessed with protecting and preserving what we have, which is a sure way of losing it. With death on our horizon we may act in ways aimed at getting it over with, ways that lead to self-destruction now simply because destruction seems inevitable. But when we envision a horizon that holds the hope of life, we are free to act without fear, free to act in truth and love and justice today because those very qualities seem to shape our own destiny.

The question of whether we are moving toward death or new life is the central question in most religious traditions, and the way a religion answers that question has powerful implications for its conception of the active life. One common formulation of the question and the answer runs something like this: We live in a world where death seems to dominate, a world that uses death as a means of power and control. Not only do we have to face our own bodily demise, but if we challenge the world's order too much, we will be threatened with anything from the death of income, or status, or reputation, to physical death by violence. As long as we live in fear

of those threats, we will live in bondage to the world. But—
and here again is the core message of all the great traditions—
we need not be afraid. Death is not the final word. Beyond
every death, large or small, there is resurrection, new life. If
we believe this and act accordingly, we will be freed from fear
and bondage, freed to live in the liberty of the Spirit.

I grew up with this traditional faith, tried to grow into it,
and for years it seemed valid to me. Like most people, I have
known both death and resurrection in my life, and until re-
cently my experience with that great cycle seemed well-
represented by the traditional formula. But then I ran across a
small book of poetry by Julia Esquivel with the stunning title
Threatened with Resurrection.[1]

Those words turned my mind upside down, and as I read
and reread the title poem of that book I realized why: I have
sometimes feared life itself, and the movement toward new
life, more than I have feared death in its various forms. In fact,
I have once or twice found life so challenging that I would
have welcomed the "relief" of some form of death. Looking
around me, I know I am not alone in this reversal of the way
things are supposed to be. Our psyches, our society, our spiritualities, seem at times to flee from life and run toward death.

There are two stories that make this point, one with humor, the other with pathos. Woody Allen, in his movie "Annie Hall," tells the story (which I embellish a bit here) of the
man who goes to a psychiatrist, complaining that his brother-
in-law, who lives with him, thinks he is a chicken. "Describe
his symptoms," the doctor says. "Maybe I can help." "Well,"
replies the man, "he cackles a lot, he pecks at the rug and the
furniture, and he makes nests in the corners." The doctor
thinks for a moment, then says, "It sounds like a simple
neurosis to me. Bring your brother-in-law in and I think I can
cure him *completely.*" "Oh, no, Doc," says the man, "we
wouldn't want that! We need the eggs!"

Here is a man who finds his brother-in-law's neurosis so
useful that he wants to preserve at least part of it. We some-

times do that to ourselves, clinging to our pathologies in full or in part because they are perversely useful to us. Some of us prefer these "little deaths" to robust health because "we need the eggs." We find our debilities functional, even comforting, and somewhere deep inside we are threatened by health, new life, resurrection.

The same point is made more somberly by an apocryphal tale about the apostle Peter. Immediately after the crucifixion and resurrection of Jesus, Peter—filled with the power of this great event—sees a blind beggar crouched in the dust beside the gate of the city. Overcome with compassion, Peter rushes to the man, places his hands over the blind eyes, and says, "In the name of the resurrected Christ, may your sight be restored!"

The beggar leaps to his feet, eyes wide open and clearly healed. But with his face full of rage he screams at Peter, "You fool! You have destroyed my way of making a living!" and in one swift and violent motion the beggar gouges out his eyes with his own thumbs and collapses into the street.[2] Here is a powerful metaphor, I think. We sometimes know how to "make a living" from our figurative blindness, but are afraid that we would starve to death if our sight were restored.

My own experience with favoring death over life includes several struggles with depression. Depression is a dreadful thing, not to be recommended for the lessons it has to teach, but if one suffers from it, then learning those lessons is the only way to get through the experience. One of my most difficult lessons involved the fact that part of me wanted to stay depressed, despite the pain and despair, because as long as I was depressed life became "easier." In my depression, no one expected much of me, and neither did I. I received more sympathy and fewer challenges. I had a legitimate reason for hiding out from the world of action and decision and responsibility. I do not mean to imply that depression is some sort of vacation, but its very hideousness makes it all the more startling that a part of me wanted to stay depressed (which, I am told, is true for some other sufferers as well).

So in my mid-life I have to say that the spiritual formula that made so much sense when I was younger ("Death threatens, but be not afraid, for resurrection is at hand") has a flip side that is equally true. Death in various forms is sometimes comforting, while resurrection and new life can be demanding and threatening. If I lived as if resurrection were real, and allowed myself to die for the sake of new life, what might I be called upon to do? What strange and difficult tasks might be laid upon me, what comforts taken away? How might my life be changed? Would I still have "the eggs," still be able to "make a living?"

For years I shared the common Christian notion that Jesus' greatest courage was in his willingness to go to his death on the cross. But now I am not so sure. His life was a continual struggle, and the thought of death may have been restful. Perhaps his greater courage was to accept resurrection—after all, sitting at the right hand of God for all eternity is hardly a job without burdens.

If we have a side that is fearful of life and attracted to death, it would help explain why our world seems so dominated by death and its agents. Why do we go so easily to war, even in an age when doomsday weapons could destroy all life? Why are we so drawn to "entertainment" that involves depictions of violence and killing? Why do we so readily embrace the notion that there are "acceptable levels of death" from carcinogenic chemicals and nuclear power plants? Perhaps because we are afraid of life, of its challenges and demands for change. Perhaps because we perversely prefer the safe and predictable confines of the grave.

We can even find this fear of life, this attraction to death, in the same spiritual traditions that preach a gospel of resurrection. There are strands of Christian faith, to take my own tradition as an example, whose distrust of the life-force is so great that their main agenda has become the control of the human spirit rather than its liberation. In these quarters, human vitality is seen as little more than a threat to good order. But the life-affirming faith of every authentic spirituality is expressed by these words from the Hebrew Bible: "I set before you life or death, blessing or curse. Choose life . . . " (Deut. 30:19, JB). If we are to follow this command and act on behalf of life, not death, we must come to terms with how and why we are "threatened with resurrection."

II. WHO THREATENS US?

Julia Esquivel, in her collection of poems *Threatened With Resurrection,* speaks in a voice that we North Americans especially need to hear. Esquivel was an elementary-school teacher in Guatemala, her native land, when her commitment to justice put her on the wrong side of Guatemala's fascist government, and Esquivel was forced into exile from the land she loves. Esquivel speaks from personal experience of many kinds of oppression: as a citizen of the third world, a Latin American, a woman, an advocate for children. The hope in her poetry is not facile, but hard-won.

The title poem from her book is long and somewhat complex, but powerful and rich in meaning. It contains several references to Guatemala's history and culture that Esquivel generously footnotes, knowing that many of her North American readers will be ignorant of these things. We will understand the poem better if we review those references briefly here. Rabinal is a town where a military massacre of peasants took place. In 1954 a mercenary army reportedly backed by our CIA overthrew the elected government of President Jacobo Arbenz (who planned to return land occupied by the United Fruit Company to the people). Since that time military regimes have been in power continuously, and the repression has been relentless; over 100,000 citizens have been murdered. The quetzal is a rare and beautiful tropical bird, the national symbol of Guatemala, that dies when it is caged, a bird that some people liken to the legendary Egyptian phoenix that rises from its own ashes. Ixcan is a mineral-rich area where Indian peasants have been driven off their native land by the wealthy and powerful.

"They Have Threatened Us With Resurrection"

It isn't the noise in the streets
that keeps us from resting, my friend,
nor is it the shouts of the young people
coming out drunk from "St. Paul's" bar,
nor is it the tumult of those who pass by excitedly
on their way to the mountains.

There is something here within us
which doesn't let us sleep,
which doesn't let us rest,
which doesn't stop pounding
deep inside,
it is the silent, warm weeping
of Indian women without their husbands,
it is the sad gaze of the children
fixed there beyond memory,
in the very pupil of our eyes
which during sleep,
though closed, keep watch
with each contraction
of the heart,
in every awakening.

Now six of them have left us,
and nine in Rabinal,
and two, plus two, plus two,
and ten, a hundred, a thousand,
a whole army
witness to our pain,
our fear,
our courage,
our hope!

What keeps us from sleeping
is that they have threatened us with Resurrection!

Because at each nightfall
though exhausted from the endless inventory
of killings since 1954,
yet we continue to love life
and do not accept their death!

They have threatened us with Resurrection
because we have felt their inert bodies
and their souls penetrated ours
doubly fortified.
Because in this marathon of Hope,
there are always others to relieve us
in bearing the courage necessary
to arrive at the goal
which lies beyond death.

They have threatened us with Resurrection
because they will not be able to wrest from us
their bodies,
their souls,
their strength,
their spirit,
nor even their death
and least of all their life.
Because they live
today, tomorrow and always
on the streets, baptized with their blood
and in the air which gathered up their cry,
in the jungle that hid their shadows,
in the river that gathered up their laughter,
in the ocean that holds their secrets,
in the craters of the volcanoes,
Pyramids of the New Day
which swallowed up their ashes.

They have threatened us with Resurrection,
because they are more alive than ever before,
because they transform our agonies,
and fertilize our struggle,
because they pick us up when we fall,
and gird us like giants
before the fear of those demented gorillas.

They have threatened us with Resurrection
because they do not know life (poor things!).

That is the whirlwind
which does not let us sleep,
the reason why asleep, we keep watch,
and awake, we dream.

No, it's not the street noises,
nor the shouts from the drunks in "St. Paul's" bar,
nor the noise from the fans at the ball park.
It is the internal cyclone of a kaleidoscopic struggle
which will heal that wound of the quetzal
fallen in Ixcan.
It is the earthquake soon to come that will shake the world
and put everything in its place.

No, brother,
it is not the noise in the streets
which does not let us sleep.

Accompany us then on this vigil
and you will know what it is to dream!
You will then know
how marvelous it is
to live threatened with Resurrection!

To dream awake,
to keep watch asleep,
to live while dying
and to already know oneself
resurrected![3]

The poem evokes several urgent and fruitful questions, one of which arises immediately with the title. Who threatens us with resurrection? At first, the answer seems obvious. The people who threaten us with resurrection are the same people who threaten us with death. In the case of the Guatemalans, the threat comes from the "demented gorillas" who do the killing on behalf of the government and its wealthy backers. Who else could threaten us with resurrection except those who want us to die?

But that notion is confounded by Esquivel's first use of the phrase "They have threatened us with Resurrection" in the body of the poem. This comes immediately after she speaks of the hundreds of peasants killed in Rabinal, and it is followed by her statement, ". . . We have felt their inert bodies / and their souls penetrated ours . . . " Here it would seem that we are threatened with resurrection not by the killers but by the dead themselves.

But this notion is itself confounded when Esquivel says, "They have threatened us with Resurrection / because they will not be able to wrest from us / their bodies, / their souls, / their strength, / their spirit, / nor even their death / and least of all their life." If "they" are the dead, why would they want to wrest their legacy from the living? Here it seems once again that it is the killers who threaten us with resurrection.

But Esquivel also makes references to "them" that are simply ambiguous in and of themselves. For example, she says, ". . . yet we continue to love life / and do not accept their death!" What does she mean by "their death?" The death of the peasants killed in Rabinal, or the death dealt out by those who killed them? Later on, the poet says, "They have threatened us with Resurrection / because they do not know life (poor things!)." Is "poor things!" a jaunty reference to those who have died and who now know something better than earthly life—or is it a gibing reference to those who show, by killing others, that they know nothing of life?

The longer that one dwells on the poem, the harder it is to say exactly who threatens us with resurrection. The poem itself is like the kaleidoscope whose image Esquivel uses; each time you turn it a new pattern appears. So the poem imitates life, in which the "threat of Resurrection" comes both from those who dispense death and from those who have died in the hope of new life. In the Gospel story, the threat of resurrection comes partly from Jesus, who accepted not only his death but his resurrection as well. But it also comes from Judas, who sent Jesus to both his death and his new life.

Esquivel, with her kaleidoscopic language, is doing what all good poets do—immersing us in life's ambiguities, refusing to give us a simplified and falsely comforting portrayal of the world in which we act.

If it is true that both the killers and the killed threaten us with resurrection, then we, the living, are caught between a rock and a hard place. On the one hand, we fear the killers, but not simply because they want to kill us. We fear them because they test our convictions about resurrection, they test our willingness to be brought into a larger life than the one we now know. On the other hand, we fear the innocent victims of the killers, those who have died for love and justice and peace. Though they are our friends, we fear them because they call us to follow them in "this marathon of Hope." If we were to take their calling seriously, we ourselves would have to undergo some form of dying.

Caught between the killers and the killed, we (those who want to live and let live) have no easy relations except sometimes with each other. So we huddle together in a conspiracy of silence, trying to ignore both the dead and their murderers, trying to ignore the ambiguous call of the new life that lies beyond death. Julia Esquivel is trying to break up our little huddle, I think, trying to inspire our active lives, calling us to engage the demented gorillas as well as our martyred friends, calling us to walk into our fear of resurrection and to open ourselves to the life on the other side.

All this ambiguity finally seems profoundly reassuring to me. It suggests that all forces in life, those of death as well as of life, may work ultimately for good, whether they intend to or not. Ultimately, both the gorillas and the martyrs act toward the same end, the end of new life through resurrection (although the gorillas, with their insensitivity to life, may never realize that grace). In their encounter both the killers and the killed "fertilize our struggle," as Esquivel says with an image of life's fecundity.

This is the same paradoxical truth that the angel in Buber's tale had to learn, or relearn, at such expense: "... that the earth must be nourished with decay and covered with shadows that its seeds may bring forth ... that souls must be made fertile with flood and sorrow, that through them the Great Work may be born." The paradox may seem difficult and discouraging on the surface. But when we begin to live it out, we experience more comfort by far than when we try to live in the illusion that we can evade our dying.

The drama that Julia Esquivel portrays in her poem is not only about the interplay of the killers and the killed. It embraces us, the living bystanders, as well, the "us" in the poem's title. The question is whether we can internalize life's ambiguous interplay of light and shadow, life and death, and learn to live in the creative center of this paradox so that through us the Great Work might be born. We will be strengthened in that task by Esquivel's insight into the nature of "resurrection."

III. THE MEANING OF RESURRECTION

It is not easy to grasp the meaning of that crucial word in this poem, partly because it points to a mystery, partly because the word is so encrusted with misinterpretation. "Resurrection" is sometimes used so literally as to suggest a civic afterlife in the sort of heaven that would have a mayor and a city council. Sometimes the word is used as a political safety valve to vent the pressures of injustice by promising oppressed people "pie in the sky when you die by and by." Sometimes the word is discarded by secularists who cannot see the poetry of the material world.

For Esquivel, I believe, resurrection is a profoundly material affair. Her vision reminds me of the basic fact of physics that nothing in the universe is ever lost, that the universe today contains the same number of atoms it had at the beginning. That simple fact is also poetry at its best, constantly illustrated (though rarely appreciated) in everyday life. When a log burns in the fireplace it does not disappear, but only changes form. Its basic particles change from seemingly solid matter to invisible waves of energy; they leave one constellation of reality only to be woven into another.

Perhaps it is something like this that Esquivel means by resurrection. As the burning log lives on in the form of energy, so also do those who die for truth live on. The question is whether we, the living, can understand that transformation and gather around the fire, allowing it to warm and energize our lives so that we can participate in resurrection and in the new life it brings.

This interpretation of Esquivel's view of resurrection is warranted in part by her repeated material imagery. Look at the places where the poet says the dead live on, "today, tomorrow, and always": on the streets, in the air, in the jungles and rivers and oceans, in the volcanic craters. These are not metaphors. They are the physical locations where the innocent were killed, as the poem makes clear—"on the streets, baptized with their blood," "in the ocean that holds their secrets," "in the craters of the volcanoes . . . which swallowed up their ashes." In these ordinary physical locations the mysterious transformation begins, a transformation of life into death and back to life again. It is a transformation that becomes complete only as we, the living, enter into it.

Some of us in North America will not understand this vision of resurrection, or be able to participate in it, until we overcome the separation, sometimes the opposition, between God and nature that we have been taught. Our theology has often put God over and against nature and has opposed anything that smacks of "nature worship." The intent of this theology was to honor the *otherness* of God, as contrasted with the *fallenness* of the natural world. But it has often functioned merely to bulwark the notion that we humans, with God on our side, have the authority to dominate nature and bring it under our control.

Theological debate aside, we are learning today on a practical level how disastrous our "stewardship" of nature has been. We are beginning to recover a sense of nature's holiness, of God within nature as well as God beyond nature, of the need to show the reverence to land, water, and air that we show to God. Only as this recovery continues will we be inspired to participate in the healing of the earth, and only so—if Esquivel is right—will we be able to participate in the great cycle of death and resurrection.

What steps can we take toward this participation? The first, and most obvious, is to go to those places where the dead lost their lives, places we would normally avoid for the pain they bring us. Once there, we must be willing to experience the void created by death, for only as we allow death to hollow us out will we be filled with life's presence.

These are steps that a counselor might urge upon any survivor so that grief could do its work. Do not avoid the places where the dead person once lived, the places where you knew life together with that person. Go there and be there; allow yourself to feel the anguish of utter loss. Only as you do so will you have a chance of being touched by the spirit of the dead one. Only so will you begin to understand that physical absence may yield a sense of presence more palpable than the body itself. Only so may you learn that life is never finally lost, only transformed.

But for Julia Esquivel, such counsel is aimed not only at personal healing for the bereaved but at political empowerment for the community as well. This is how we join the "marathon of Hope" in which Esquivel calls us to become runners, a marathon in which we move together toward the goal "which lies beyond death." But that goal, that resurrection, is not the arising of the individual from the dead as we, in our individualism, have so often imagined it to be. Esquivel's image of resurrection involves an entire people arising as one and becoming a community in which injustice is no more. If we do our grieving deeply and well, we become participants in a communal uprising, a resurrection in which the dead live on through the commitment of the survivors. Through the bonds of community, death is transformed into energy for life, and ultimately our losses are overcome.

For Esquivel, there is no resurrection of isolated individuals. She is simply not concerned about private resurrections, yours or mine or her own. Each of us is resurrected only as we enter into the network of relationships called community, a network that embraces not only living persons but people who have died, and nonhuman creatures as well. Resurrection has personal significance—if we understand the person as a communal being—but it is above all a corporate, social, and political event, an event in which justice and truth and love come to fruition.

For Esquivel, resurrection seems also to be an apocalyptic event: "It is the earthquake soon to come that will shake the world / and put everything in its place." She seems to be speaking in ancient end-time language about a vast and ongoing process that will do its work with or without us, but one which we are called to acknowledge and join as a sign of our own relation to reality.

The root meaning of the word *apocalypse* is to uncover, to reveal. So apocalyptic language is simply another way of referring to the contemplative process in which illusion is stripped away and reality revealed. That is what an earthquake does; it uncovers the illusion that we are standing on solid ground and reveals the reality of hidden strains and faults. Though an earthquake damages the surface structures of our lives, its power is generated by misalignments within the earth that must be returned to right order. For Esquivel, that means the resurrection order of community between nature, persons, nations, and God—an order that relieves the stresses of injustice.

"Accompany us then on this vigil," Esquivel calls out. "You will then know / how marvelous it is / to live threatened with Resurrection!" Here the apocalyptic imagery deepens, for in classical practice a vigil is a watch kept during the night, a steady scanning of the horizon for the first hints of light. In keeping vigil we peer into the darkness, seeking signs of the new day that will bring an end to injustice and gather us into the beloved community.

IV. RESURRECTION INTO COMMUNITY

Having explored what resurrection is and who threatens us with it, I want to look again at the nature of the "threat." I want to try to understand how Julia Esquivel can say with such enthusiasm, "how marvelous it is / to live threatened with Resurrection!"

If we take Esquivel seriously, and the experience she represents, the threat of resurrection for people like me seems clear. It is a threat aimed at those of us who have some measure of power by virtue of the simple facts that we are alive, that we have food and clothing and housing, that we are gifted with education and work and income, and that we are therefore capable of acting on behalf of the millions of people who are unjustly deprived of these blessings. If we—people like me and perhaps you—really believed in resurrection, believed it not just in theory but in our bones, we would have no choice but to risk all that we have by taking action for justice.

Bone-deep knowledge of resurrection would take away the fears that some of us presently use to justify our cautious, self-protective lives. Death-dealing fear would be replaced by life-giving faith, and we would be called to do God-knows-what for God-knows-who. Perhaps we would be compelled to take in a homeless person; to go to prison in protest of nuclear madness; to leave jobs that contribute to violence; to "speak truth to power" in a hundred risky ways. In the process, we might lose much that we have, perhaps even our lives—and that is the threat of resurrection.

I remember an occasion when I came face-to-face with one of the "demented gorillas" about whom Esquivel writes, an occasion when the fear in my bones was stronger than the faith. A university near my home invited a colonel in the Army of the Philippines to speak on campus. After the invitation was extended it became known that Amnesty International had evidence that this colonel frequently participated in the torture of civilians during the Marcos regime. Several of us decided to conduct a nonviolent protest at the site of the lecture, so we stood silently at the back of the hall with posters naming this man's crimes against humanity. In the process, we drew the attention of the media to the issue and, of course, to ourselves.

I was on my turf, not his; I was in an American academic hall, not the interrogation shack of a Filipino army post; I was protected by the Bill of Rights, not subject to the whims of the colonel's cruelty. But still I was afraid. It was frightening to hear this man blithely deny torture one moment, then say that "it sometimes happens," then admit that his unit had "borrowed" a woman activist for a day of "questioning," then brush off a question about electrical shock torture with the mumbled aside, "I have more sophisticated methods than that." I was well-protected from him, and yet I felt from him the threat of resurrection. How much more threatening resurrection would have been if I had been vulnerable to his malicious power.

How, then, is Julia Esquivel able to claim that it is "marvelous" to live threatened with resurrection? Obviously, she knows something bone-deep that I do not, so I can only guess. But her words, and the faith that lies behind them, lead me to suggest two answers to the question.

First, since death is our constant companion whether we like it or not, it must be "marvelous" to live in a dialogue with death in which life gets the final word. Esquivel praises what it means "to live while dying / and to already know oneself / resurrected!" It is a simple fact that we live while dying, that every minute of life brings us a minute closer to death. But our encounter with that fact is painful at first, and there is much in us that wants to evade the pain by denying death as long as we can.

When we live in illusion, denying reality, resisting the inevitable, we live in a tension that drains us of energy without our even knowing it. So if we try to gain life by denying death, the paradoxical result is that we become lifeless. This is why "disillusionment" is so important, for by losing our illusions we can tap the energy of the reality that lies beyond them. Once we are thoroughly disillusioned we can say, with Thoreau, "Reality is fabulous!" No matter how difficult reality may be, it contains more life than any illusion.

This is one sense, I think, in which Julia Esquivel is able to say that it is "marvelous" to live under the threat of resurrection. The reality is that sooner or later all we have will be taken from us by death. But if we can live with the threat of resurrection in our bones, then we will live truly and well. Then we will join in a corporate witness that is immortal, a witness that is only strengthened by the forces of death, a witness that is in itself the resurrection life.

If the importance of accepting the reality of death is the first reason why Esquivel finds it "marvelous" to live threatened with resurrection, the second reason is the paradox of the first. Only by accepting and entering into death can we know true life. Or—to put it into words that cannot be improved upon—only when we lose our lives will we find them.

When Jesus spoke those words, he was not exhorting people toward something they "ought" to do, but simply articulating a basic law of life. As long as we cling to life as we understand it, we cling to a pinched and deadly image of things, an image heavily conditioned by our egos, our social programming, our limited knowledge of the options. But when we are willing to let go of life as we want it to be and allow the larger reality to live in and through us instead, then in our dying we come alive. This is the truth that Julia Esquivel voices when she says of those Guatemalans who have died in the struggle for justice that "they are more alive than ever before."

For many of us, the life we need to lose is life lived in the image of the autonomous self, and the life we shall then find is that of the self embedded in community—a community that connects us not only to other people but to the natural world as well. No wonder resurrection is so threatening; it forces us to abandon any illusion we may have that we are in charge of our own lives, able to do whatever we want, accountable to no one but ourselves, free of responsibility to others. Resurrection requires that we replace that illusion with the reality that we rise and fall together, that we have no choice but to live in and with and for the entire community of creation.

But Esquivel knows that as we abandon our individualism and accept our membership in community, a "marvelous" thing happens. We become less afraid, more at home on earth, because we no longer stand alone. Resurrection into community saves us from the secret fear of the autonomous self that he or she is doomed to be forever alone, to carry the whole load. What a joy it would be to know, with Julia Esquivel, that "there are always others to relieve us / in bearing the courage necessary / to arrive at the goal / which lies beyond death."

Paradoxically, as we enter more deeply into the true community of our lives, we are relieved of those fears that keep us from becoming the authentic selves we were born to be. Community and individuality are not an either/or choice, any more than life and death are. Instead, they are the poles of another great paradox. A culture of isolated individualism produces mass conformity because people who think they must bear life all alone are too fearful to take the risks of selfhood. But people who know that they are embedded in an eternal community are both freed and empowered to become who they were born to be.

In the active life of work, creativity, and caring we are given endless opportunities to lose ourselves so that we may find ourselves, to join with others in the great community so that, freed from the fear of isolation, we may become who we are. It is the testimony of Julia Esquivel that by joyfully embracing the threat of resurrection we can work, create, and care in ways that take us not toward the futility of death but toward the fullness of new life for ourselves and for the whole of creation.

Notes

CHAPTER 1

1. The best analysis I know of the history of active and contemplative life is Hannah Arendt, *The Human Condition* (Garden City, NY: Doubleday Anchor Books, 1959).
2. Joseph Campbell, *The Power of Myth* (NY: Doubleday, 1988), 5. Thomas Merton makes a similar point in *A Vow of Conversation* (NY: Farrar, Straus & Giroux, 1988), 159.
3. Barry Lopez, *Crossing Open Ground* (NY: Charles Scribner's Sons, 1988), 69.

CHAPTER 2

1. Niels Bohr, quoted in Avery Dulles, *The Reshaping of Catholicism* (San Francisco: Harper & Row, 1989).
2. John Howard Griffin, *Black Like Me* (Boston: Houghton Mifflin, 1961).
3. Thomas Merton, *The Hidden Ground of Love* (NY: Farrar, Straus & Giroux, 1985), 454ff.
4. Dylan Thomas, "Do Not Go Gentle Into That Good Night," in *The Poems of Dylan Thomas* (NY: New Directions, 1971), 207.
5. See "The Fortunate Fall," in Walter A. Elwell, ed., *Evangelical Dictionary of Theology* (Grand Rapids, MI: Baker Book House, 1984), 423–24.
6. Theodore Roethke, "The Waking," in *The Collected Poems of Theodore Roethke* (London: Faber & Faber, 1966), 108.
7. Rainer Maria Rilke, *Letters to a Young Poet,* trans. by Stephen Mitchell (NY: Vintage Books, 1987), 78.
8. Thomas Merton, "Hagia Sophia," in Thomas P. McDonnell, ed., *A Thomas Merton Reader* (NY: Doubleday, 1974), 506.
9. Annie Dillard, *Teaching a Stone to Talk* (NY: Harper & Row, 1982), 94–95.

CHAPTER 3

1. Eli Wiesel, quoted by Rachel Adler, "The Virgin in the Brothel and Other Anomalies: Character and Context in the Legend of Beruriah," *Tikkun,* 3 (November/December 1988): 28.
2. Martin Buber, quoted in "Sunbeams," *The Sun,* (July 1989): 40.
3. Thomas Merton, *The Way of Chuang Tzu* (NY: New Directions, 1969).
4. Merton, "Active Life," in *The Way of Chuang Tzu,* 141–142.
5. John McKnight, "Professionalized Service and Disabling Help," in Ivan Illich *et al.,* eds., *Disabling Professions* (London: Marion Boyars, Inc., 1977), 69–91.
6. Alan W. Watts, "Western Mythology: Its Dissolution and Transformation," in Joseph Campbell, ed., *Myths, Dreams, and Religion* (Dallas, TX: Spring Publications, 1988), 11.
7. David Macaulay, *Great Moments in Architecture* (Boston: Houghton Mifflin, 1978), Plate XI.

CHAPTER 4

1. Thomas Merton, "The Woodcarver," in *The Way of Chuang Tzu,* 110–111.
2. Merton, "The Need to Win," in *The Way of Chuang Tzu,* 107.
3. See, for example, Richard N. Bolles, *What Color Is Your Parachute?* (Berkeley, CA: Ten Speed Press, 1981).
4. Thomas Merton, "Cutting Up an Ox," in *The Way of Chuang Tzu,* 45–47.

CHAPTER 5

1. Martin Buber, *Tales of Angels, Spirits, and Demons,* trans. by David Antin and Jerome Rothenberg (NY: Hawk's Well Press, 1958), 9–11. The tale is also collected in Howard Schwartz, ed., *Imperial Messages* (NY: Avon Books, 1976), 113–114.
2. Buber, *Tales of Angels,* 9–11.
3. For more about this remarkable man, see Stanley Vishnewski, *Wings of the Dawn* (NY: The Catholic Worker, undated).
4. Nikos Kazantzakis, *The Last Temptation of Christ,* trans. by Peter A. Bien (NY: Simon and Schuster, 1960).

CHAPTER 6

1. Paul J. Achtemeier, ed., *Harper's Bible Dictionary* (San Francisco: Harper & Row, 1985), 712.
2. Willie Nelson, *Black Rose,* on Willie Nelson, *Me and Paul* (Spicewood, TX: Willie Nelson Music Co., 1971). Sound recording.
3. Paul J. Achtemeier, ed., *Harper's Bible Dictionary,* 220.
4. John Bartlett, *Familiar Quotations* (Boston: Little, Brown, 1955), 932.
5. Henri J. M. Nouwen, "Temptation," *Sojourners,* 10 (July 1981): 25–27.
6. Nouwen, "Temptation," 25–27.
7. Nouwen, "Temptation," 25–27.
8. Rilke, *Letters to a Young Poet,* 97.

CHAPTER 7

1. Black Elk, quoted in Richard Kehl, *Silver Departures* (La Jolla, CA: The Green Tiger Press, 1983), 8.
2. The best book that I know on community is Jean Vanier, *Community and Growth* (NY: Paulist Press, 1979).

CHAPTER 8

1. Julia Esquivel, *Threatened With Resurrection* (Elgin, IL: The Brethren Press, 1982).
2. I have never seen this story in print, though I have heard it told by several people. I have no idea when or where it originated.
3. Julia Esquivel, *Threatened With Resurrection,* 59–63.